Observation Posts

Observation Posts
The Letters of an Artillery Officer on the Western Front During the Great War

Carry On

Living Bayonets

Coningsby Dawson

LEONAUR

Observation Posts
The Letters of an Artillery Officer on the Western Front During the Great War
Carry On and *Living Bayonets*
by Coningsby Dawson

First published under the titles
Carry On
and
Living Bayonets

Leonaur is an imprint
of Oakpast Ltd

ISBN: 978-0-85706-743-2 (hardcover)
ISBN: 978-0-85706-744-9 (softcover)

http://www.leonaur.com

Publisher's Notes

The opinions of the authors represent a view of events in which he
was a participant related from his own perspective,
as such the text is relevant as an historical document.

The views expressed in this book are not necessarily
those of the publisher.

Contents

Carry On

CONINGSBY DAWSON

Contents

Introduction

The letters in this volume were not written for publication. They are intimate and personal in a high degree. They would not now be published by those to whom they are addressed, had they not come to feel that the spirit and temper of the writer might do something to strengthen and invigorate those who, like himself, are called on to make great sacrifices for high causes and solemn duties.

They do not profess to give any new information about the military operations of the Allies; this is the task of the publicist, and at all times is forbidden to the soldier in the field. Here and there some striking or significant fact has been allowed to pass the censor; but the value of the letters does not lie in these things. It is found rather in the record of how the dreadful yet heroic realities of war affect an unusually sensitive mind, long trained in moral and romantic idealism; the process by which this mind adapts itself to unanticipated and incredible conditions, to acts and duties which lie close to horror, and are only saved from being horrible by the efficacy of the spiritual effort which they evoke.

Hating the brutalities of war, clearly perceiving the wide range of its cruelties, yet the heart of the writer is never hardened by its daily commerce with death; it is purified by pity and terror, by heroism and sacrifice, until the whole nature seems fresh annealed into a finer strength.

The intimate nature of these letters makes it necessary to say something about the writer.

11

Coningsby Dawson graduated with honours in history from Oxford in 1905, and in the same year came to the United States with the intention of taking a theological course at Union Seminary. After a year at the Seminary he reached the conclusion that his true lifework lay in literature, and he at once began to fit himself for his vocation. In the meantime his family left England, and we had made our home in Taunton, Massachusetts, Here, in a quiet house, amid lawns and leafy elms, he gave himself with indefatigable ardour to the art of writing. He wrote from seven to ten hours a day, producing many poems, short stories, and three novels.

Few writers have ever worked harder to attain literary excellence, or have practised a more austere devotion to their art. I often marvelled how a young man, fresh from a brilliant career at the greatest of English Universities, could be content with a life that was so widely separated from association with men and affairs. I wondered still more at the patience with which he endured the rebuffs that always await the beginner in literature, and the humility with which he was willing to learn the hard lessons of his apprenticeship in literary form.

The secret lay, no doubt, in his secure sense of a vocation, and his belief that good work could not fail in the end to justify itself. But, not the less, these four years of obscure drudgery wore upon his spirit, and hence some of the references in these letters to his days of self-despising. The period of waiting came to an end at last with the publication in 1913 of his *Garden Without Walls*, which attained immediate success. When he speaks in these letters of his brief burst of fame, he refers to those crowded months in the Fall of 1913, when his novel was being discussed on every hand, and, for the first time, he met many writers of established reputation as an equal.

Another novel. *The Raft*, followed *The Garden Without Walls*. The nature of his life now seemed fixed. To the task of novel-writing he had brought a temperament highly idealistic and romantic, a fresh and vivid imagination, and a thorough literary equipment. His life, as he planned it, held but one purpose for him, outside the warmth and tenacity of its affections—the triumph of the efficient purpose in the adequate expression of his mind in literature. The austerity of his long years of preparation had left him relatively indifferent to the common prizes of life, though they had done nothing to lessen his intense joy in life.

His whole mind was concentrated on his art. His adventures would be the adventures of the mind in search of ampler modes of expression. His crusades would be the crusades of the spirit in search of the realities of truth. He had received the public recognition which gave him faith in himself and faith in his ability to achieve the reputation of the true artist, whose work is not cheapened but dignified and broadened by success. So he read the future, and so his critics read it for him. And then, sudden and unheralded, there broke on this quiet life of intellectual devotion the great storm of 1914. The guns that roared along the Marne shattered all his purposes, and left him face to face with a solemn spiritual exigency which ad mitted no equivocation.

At first, in common with multitudes more experienced than himself, he did not fully comprehend the true measure of the cataclysm which had overwhelmed the world. There had been wars before, and they had been fought out by standing armies. It was incredible that any war should last more than a few months. Again and again the world had been assured that war would break down with its own weight, that no war could be financed beyond a certain brief period, that the very nature of modern warfare, with its terrible engines of destruction, made swift decisions a necessity.

The conception of a British War which involved the entire manhood of the nation was new, and unparalleled in past history. And the further conception of a war so vast in its issues that it really threatened the very existence of the nation was new too. Alarmists had sometimes predicted these things, but they had been disbelieved. Historians had used such phrases of long past struggles, but often as a mode of rhetoric rather than as the expression of exact truth. Yet, in a very few weeks, it became evident that not alone England, but the entire fabric of liberal civilisation was threatened by a power that knew no honour, no restraints of either caution or magnanimity, no ethic but the armed might that trampled under blood-stained feet all the things which the common sanction of centuries held dearest and fairest.

Perhaps, if Coningsby had been resident in England, these realities of the situation would have been immediately apparent. Residing in America, the real outlines of the struggle were a little dimmed by distance. Nevertheless, from the very first he saw clearly where his duty lay. He could not enlist immediately. He was bound in honour to fulfil various literary obligations. His latest book, *Slaves of Freedom*, was in process of being adapted for serial use, and its publication would follow.

He set the completion of this work as the period when he must enlist; working on with difficult self-restraint toward the appointed hour. If he had regrets for a career broken at the very point where it had reached success and was assured of more than competence, he never expressed them. His one regret was the effect of his enlistment on those most closely bound to him by affections which had been deepened and made more tender by the sense of common exile.

At last the hour came when he was free to follow the imperative call of patriotic duty. He went to Ottawa, saw Sir Sam Hughes, and was offered a commission in the Canadian Field Artillery on the completion of his training at the Royal Military College, at Kingston, Ontario. The last weeks of his training were passed at the military camp of Petewawa on the Ottawa River. There his family was able to meet him in the July of 1916. While we were with him he was selected, with twenty-four other officers, for immediate service in France; and at the same time his two younger brothers enlisted in the Naval Patrol, then being recruited in Canada by Commander Armstrong.

The letters in this volume commence with his departure from Ottawa. Week by week they have come, with occasional interruptions; mud-stained epistles, written in pencil, in dug-outs by the light of a single candle, in the brief moments snatched from hard and perilous duties. They give no hint of where he was on the far-flung battle-line. We know now that he was at Albert, at Thiepval, at Courcelette, and at the taking of the Regina trench, where, unknown to him, one of his cousins fell in the heroic charge of the Canadian infantry. His constant thoughtfulness for those who were left at home is manifest in all he writes. It has been expressed also in other ways, dear and precious to remember: in flowers delivered by his order from the battlefield each Sabbath morning at our house in Newark, in cables of birthday congratulations, which arrived on the exact date. Nothing has been forgotten that could alleviate the loneliness of our separation, or stimulate our courage, or make us conscious of the unbroken bond of love.

The general point of view in these letters is, I think, adequately expressed in the phrase "Carry On," which I have used as the title of this book. It was our happy lot to meet Coningsby in London in the January of the present year, when he was granted ten days' leave. In the course of conversation one night he laid emphasis on the fact that he, and those who served with him, were, after all, not professional soldiers, but civilians at war.

They did not love war, and when the war was ended not five *per cent* of them would remain in the army. They were men who had left professions and vocations which still engaged the best parts of their minds, and would return to them when the hour came. War was for them an occupation, not a vocation. Yet they had proved themselves, one and all, splendid soldiers, bearing the greatest hardships without complaint, and facing wounds and death with a gay courage which had made the Canadian forces famous even among a host of men, equally brave and heroic.

The secret of their fortitude lay in the one brief phrase, "Carry On." Their fortitude was of the spirit rather than the nerves. They were aware of the solemn ideals of justice, liberty, and righteousness for which they fought, and would never give up till they were won. In the completeness of their surrender to a great cause they had been lifted out of themselves to a new plane of living by the transformation of their spirit. It was the dogged indomitable drive of spiritual forces controlling bodily forces. Living or dying those forces would prevail. They would carry on to the end, however long the war, and would count no sacrifice too great to assure its triumph.

This is the spirit which breathes through these letters. The splendour of war, as my son puts it, is in nothing external; it is all in the souls of the men. "There's a marvellous grandeur about all this carnage and desolation—men's souls rise above the distress—they have to, in order to survive." "Every man I have met out here has the amazing guts to wear his crown of thorns as though it were a cap-and-bells." They have shredded off their weaknesses, and attained that "corporate stout-hearted-ness" which is "the acme of what Aristotle meant by virtue." For himself, he discovers that the plague of his former modes of life lay in self-distrust

It was the disease of the age. The doubt of many things which it were wisdom to believe had ended in the doubt of one's own capacity for heroism. All those doubts and self-despisings had vanished in the supreme surrender to sacrificial duty. The doors of the Kingdom of Heroism were flung so wide that the meanest might enter in, and in that act the humblest became comrades of Drake's men, who could jest as they died. No one knows his real strength till it is put to the test; the highest joy of life is to discover that the soul can meet the test, and survive it.

The Somme battlefield, from which all these letters were despatched, is an Inferno much more terrible than any Dante pictured. It is a vast sea of mud, full of the unburied dead, pitted and pock-marked by shell-holes, treeless and house-less, "the abomination of desolation." And the men who toil across it look more like outcasts of the London Embankment than soldiers.

"They're loaded down like pack-animals, their shoulders are rounded, they're wearied to death, but they go on and go on. . . . There's no flash of sword or splendour of uniforms. They're only very tired men determined to carry on. The war will be won by tired men who can never again pass an insurance test."

Yet they carry on—the "broken counter-jumper, the ragged

ex-plumber," the clerk from the office, the man from the farm; Londoner, Canadian, Australian, New Zealander, men drawn from every quarter of the Empire, who daily justify their manhood by devotion to an ideal and by contempt of death. And in the heart of each there is a settled conviction that the cause for which they have sacrificed so much must triumph. They have no illusions about an early peace. They see their comrades fall, and say quietly, "He's gone west."

They do heroic things daily, which in a lesser war would have won the Victoria Cross, but in this war are commonplaces. They know themselves re-born in soul, and are dimly aware that the world is travailing toward new birth with them. They are still very human, men who end their letters- with a row of crosses which stand for kisses. They are not dehumanised by war; the kindliness and tenderness of their natures are unspoiled by all their daily traffic in horror. But they have won their souls; and when the days of peace return these men will take with them to the civilian life a tonic strength and nobleness which will arrest and extirpate the decadence of society with the saving salt of valour and of faith.

It may be said also that they do not hate their foe, although they hate the things for which he fights. They are fighting a clean fight, with men: whose courage they respect. A German prisoner who comes into the British camp is sure of good. I treatment. He is neither starved nor insulted. His captors share with him cheerfully their rations and their little luxuries. Sometimes a sullen brute will spit in the face of his captor when he offers him a cigarette; he is always an officer, never a private. And occasionally between these fighting hosts there are acts of magnanimity which stand out illumined against the dark background of death and suffering.

One of the stories told me by my son illustrates this. During one fierce engagement a British officer saw a German officer impaled on the barbed wire, writhing in anguish. The fire was dreadful, yet he still hung there unscathed. At length the British officer could stand it no longer. He said quietly, "I can't bear to look at that poor chap any longer." So he went out under the hail of shell, released him, took him on his shoulders and carried him to the German trench. The firing ceased. Both sides watched the act with wonder. Then the commander in the German trench came forward, took from his own bosom the Iron Cross, and pinned it on the breast of the British officer. Such an episode is true to the holiest ideals of chivalry; and it is all the more welcome because the German record is stained by so many acts of barbarism, which the world cannot forgive.

This magnanimous attitude toward the enemy is very apparent in these letters. The man whose mind is filled with great ideals of sacrifice and duty has no room for the narrowness of hate. He can pity a foe whose sufferings exceed his own, and the more so because he knows that his foe is doomed. The British troops do know this to-day by many infallible signs. In the early days of the war untrained men, poorly equipped with guns, were pitted against the best trained troops in Europe.

The first Canadian armies were sacrificed, as was that immortal army of Imperial troops who saved the day at Mons. The Canadians often perished in that early fighting by the excess of their own reckless bravery. They are still the most daring fighters in the British army, but they have profited by the hard discipline of the past. They know now that they have not only the will to conquer, but the means of conquest. Their artillery has become conspicuous for its efficiency. It is the ceaseless artillery fire which has turned the issue of the war for the British forces.

The work of the infantry is beyond praise. They "go over the top" with superb courage, and all who have seen them are ready to say with my son, "I'm hats off to the infantry." And in this final efficiency, surpassing all that could have been thought possible in the earlier stages of the war, the British forces read the clear augury of victory. The war will be won by the Allied armies; not only because they fight for the better cause, which counts for much, in spite of Napoleon's cynical saying that "*God is on the side of the strongest battalions*"; but because at last they have superiority in equipment, discipline and efficiency.

Upon that shell-torn Western front, amid the mud and carnage of the Somme, there has been slowly forged the weapon which will drive the Teuton enemy across the Rhine, and give back to Europe and the world unhindered liberty and enduring peace.

W. J. Dawson.

March, 1917.

The Letters

In order to make some of the allusions in these letters clear I will set down briefly the circumstances which explain them, and supply a narrative link where it may be required.

I have already mentioned the military camp at Petewawa, on the Ottawa River. The camp is situated about seven miles from Pembroke. The Ottawa River is at this point a beautiful lake. Immediately opposite the camp is a little summer hotel of the simplest description. It was at this hotel that my wife, my daughter, and myself stayed in the early days of July, 1916.

The hotel was full of the wives of the officers stationed in the camp. During the daytime I was the only man among the guests. About five o'clock in the afternoon the officers from the camp began to arrive on a primitive motor ferryboat. My son came over each day, and we often visited him at the camp. His long training at Kingston had been very severe. It included besides the various classes which he attended a great deal of hard exercise, long rides or foot marches over frozen roads before breakfast, and so forth.

After this strenuous winter the camp at Petewawa was a delightful change. His tent stood on a bluff, commanding an exquisite view of the broad stretch of water, diversified by many small islands.

We had a great deal of swimming in the lake, and several motorboat excursions to its beautiful upper reaches. One afternoon when we went over in our launch to meet him at the camp wharf, he told us that that day a general had come from Ottawa to ask for twenty-five picked officers to supply the casualties among the Canadian field artillery at the front. He had immediately volunteered and been accepted.

At this time my two younger sons, who had joined us at Petewawa in order to see their brother, enrolled themselves in the Royal Naval Motor Patrol Service, and had to return to Nelson, British Columbia, to settle their affairs. Near Nelson, on the Kootenay Lake, we have a large fruit ranch, managed by my second son, Reginald. My youngest son, Eric, was with a law-firm in Nelson, and had just passed his final examinations as solicitor and barrister.

This ranch had played a great part in our lives. The scenery is among the finest in British Columbia. We usually spent our summers there, finding not only continual interest in the development of our orchards, but a great deal of pleasure in riding, swimming, and boating.

We had often talked of building a modem house there, but had never done so. The original "little shack" was the work of Reginald's own hands, in the days when most of the ranch was primeval forest. It had been added to, but was still of the simplest description.

One reason why we had not built a modern house was that this "little shack" had become much endeared to us by association and memory. We were all together there more than once, and Coningsby had written a great deal there.

We built later on a sort of summer library—a big room on the edge of a beautiful ravine—to which reference is made in later letters. Some of the happiest days of our lives were spent in these lovely surroundings, and the memory of those blue summer days, amid the fragrance of miles of pine-forest, often recurs to Coningsby as he writes from the mud-wastes of the Somme.

We left Petewawa to go to the ranch before Coningsby sailed for England, that we might get our other two sons ready for their journey to England. They left us on August 21st, and the ranch was sub-let to Chinamen in the end of September, when we returned to Newark, New Jersey.

1

Ottawa, July 16th, 1916.

Dearest All:

So much has happened since last I saw you that it's difficult to know where to start. On Thursday, after lunch, I got the news that we were to entrain from Petewawa next Friday morning. I at once put in for leave to go to Ottawa the next day until the following Thursday at reveille. We came here with a lot of the other officers who are going over and have been having a very full time.

I am sailing from a port unknown on board the *Olympic* with 6,000 troops—there is to be a big convoy. I feel more than ever I did—and I'm sure it's a feeling that you share since visiting the camp—that I am setting out on a Crusade from which it would have been impossible to withhold myself with honour. I go quite gladly and contentedly, and pray that in God's good time we may all sit again in the little shack at Kootenay and listen to the rustling of the orchard outside. It will be of those summer days that I shall be thinking all the time.

Yours, with very much love,

Con.

2

Halifax July 23rd.

My Dear Ones:

We've spent all morning on the dock, seeing to our baggage, and have just got leave ashore for two hours. We have had letters handed to us saying that on no account are we to mention anything concerning our passage overseas, neither are we allowed to cable our arrival from the other side until four clear days have elapsed.

You are thinking of me this quiet Sunday morning at the ranch, and I of you. And I am wishing As I wish, I stop and ask myself, "Would I be there if I could have my choice?" And I remember those lines of Emerson's which you quoted:

Though love repine and reason chafe.
There comes a voice without reply,
'Twere man's perdition to be safe.
When for the Truth he ought to die.

I wouldn't turn back if I could, but my heart cries out against "the voice which speaks without reply."

Things are growing deeper with me in all sorts of ways. Family affections stand out so desirably and vivid, like meadows green after rain. And religion means more. The love of a few dear human people and the love of the divine people out of sight, are all that one has to lean on in the graver hours of life. I hope I come back again—I very much hope I come back again; there are so many finer things that I could do with the rest of my days—bigger things.

But if by any chance I should cross the seas to stay, you'll know that that also will be right and as big as anything that I could do with life, and something that you'll be able to be just as proud about as if I had lived to fulfil all your other dear hopes for me. I don't suppose I shall talk of this again. But I wanted you to know that underneath all the lightness and ambition there's something that I learnt years ago in Highbury.[1] I've become a little child again in God's hands, with full confidence in His love and wisdom, and a growing trust that whatever He decides for me will be best and kindest.

This is the last letter I shall be able to send to you before the other boys follow me. Keep brave, dear ones, for all our sakes; don't let any of us turn cowards whatever ultimately happens. We've a tradition to live up to now that we have become a family of soldiers and sailors. I shall long for the time when you come over to England. Where will our meeting be and when? Perhaps the war may be ended and then won't you be glad that we dared all this sorrow of goodbyes?

God bless and keep you,

Con.

---

1. We resided over thirteen years at Highbury, London, N., during my pastorate of the Highbury Quadrant Congregational Church.

3

Oxford

July 27th, 1916.

My Very Dear People:

Here we are scooting along across the same old Atlantic we've crossed so many times on journeys of pleasure. I'm at a loss to make my letters interesting, as we are allowed to say little concerning the voyage and everything is censored.

There are men on board who are going back to the trenches for the second time. One of them is a captain in the *Princess Pat's*, who is badly scarred in his neck and cheek and thighs, and has been in Canada recuperating. There is also a young flying chap who has also seen service. They are all such boys and so plucky in the face of certain knowledge.

This morning I woke up thinking of our motor-tour of two years ago in England, and especially of our first evening at The Three Cups in Dorset. I feel like running down there to see it all again if I get any leave on landing. How strange it will be to go back to Highbury again like this! The little boy who ran back and forth to school down Paradise Row little thought of the person who today masquerades as his elder self.

Heigho! I wish I could tell you a lot of things that I'm not allowed to. This letter would be much more interesting then.

In seventeen days the boys will also have left you—so this will arrive when you're horribly lonely. I'm so sorry for you dear people—but I'd be sorrier for you if we were all with you. If I were a father or mother, I'd rather have my sons dead than see them failing when the supreme sacrifice was called for.

I marvel all the time at the prosaic and even coarse types of men who have risen to the greatness of the occasion. And there's not a man aboard who would have chosen the job ahead of him. One man here used to pay other people to kill his pigs because he couldn't endure the cruelty of doing it himself. And now he's going to kill men. And he's a sample. I wonder if there is a Lord God of Battles—or is he only an invention of man and an excuse for man's own actions.

Monday.

We are just in—safely arrived in spite of everything. I hope you had no scare reports of our having been sunk—such reports often get about when a big troop ship is on the way.

I'm baggage master for my draft, and have to get on deck now. You'll have a long letter from me soon.

Goodbye,

Yours ever.

Con.

4

Shorncliff, August 19th, 1916.

My Dearests:

We haven't had any hint of what is going to happen to us—whether field artillery, the heavies or trench mortars. There seems little doubt that we are to be in England for a little while taking special courses.

I read father's letter yesterday. You are very brave—you never thought that you would be the father of a soldier and sailors; and, as you say, there's a kind of tradition about the way in which the fathers of soldiers and sailors should act. Confess—aren't you more honestly happy to be our father as we are now than as we were? I know quite well you are, in spite of the loneliness and heartache.

We've all been forced into a heroism of which we did not think ourselves capable. We've been carried up to the Calvary of the world where it is expedient that a few men should suffer that all the generations to come may be better.

I understand in a dim way all that you suffer—the sudden divorce of all that we had hoped for from the present—the ceaseless questionings as to what lies ahead. Your end of the business is the worse. For me, I can go forward steadily because of the greatness of the glory. I never thought to have the chance to suffer in my body for other men.

The insufficiency of merely setting nobilities down on paper is finished. How unreal I seem to myself! Can it be true that I am here and you are in the still aloofness of the Rockies? I think the multitude of my changes has blunted my perceptions.

I trudge along like a traveller between high hedgerows; my heart is blinkered so that I am scarcely aware of landscapes. My thoughts are always with you—I make calculations for the differences of time that too discourteous in its interruption of many dreams and plans and loves.

Yours with very much love,

Con.

5

Shorncliff, August 19th, 1916.

My Dears:

It's not quite three weeks today since I came to England, and it seems ages. The first week was spent on leave, the second I passed my exams in gun drill and gun-laying, and this week I have finished my riding. Next Monday I start on my gunnery.

Do you remember Captain S. at the camp? I had his young brother to dinner with me last night—he's just back from France minus an eye. He lasted three and a half weeks, and was buried four feet deep by a shell. He's a jolly boy, as cheerful as you could want and is very good company. He gave me a vivid description. He had a great boy-friend. At the start of the war they both joined, S. in the artillery, his friend in the Mounted Rifles.

At parting they exchanged identification tokens. S.'s bore his initials and the one word "Violets"—which meant that they were his favourite flower and he would like to have some scattered over him when he was buried. His friend wore his initials and the words "No flowers by request." It was S.'s first week out—they were advancing, having driven back the enemy, and were taking up a covered position in a wood from which to renew their offensive.

It was night, black as pitch, but they knew that the wood must have been the scene of fighting by the scuttling of the rats. Suddenly the moon came out, and from beneath a bush S. saw a face—or rather half a face—which he thought he recognised, gazing up at him. He corrects himself when he tells the story, and says that it wasn't so much the disfigured features as the profile that struck him as familiar. He bent down and searched beneath the shirt, and drew out a little metal disc with "No flowers by request" written on it.

I don't know whether I ought to repeat things like that to you, but the description was so graphic. I have met many who have returned from the front, and what puzzles me in all of them is their unawed acceptance of death. I don't think I could ever accept it as natural; it's too discourteous in its interruption of many dreams and plans and loves.

Yours with very much love,
Con.

6

Shorncliff, August 30th, 1916.

My Dearests:

I have just returned from sending you a cable to let you know that I'm off to France. The word came out in orders yesterday, and I shall leave before the end of the week with a draft of officers—I have been in England just a day over four weeks. My only regret is that I shall miss the boys who should be travelling up to London about the same time as I am setting out for the front. After I have been there for three months I am supposed to get a leave—this should be due to me about the beginning of December, and you can judge how I shall count on it. Think of the meeting with R. and E., and the immensity of the joy.

Selfishly I wish that you were here at this moment—actually I'm glad that you are away. Everybody goes out quite unemotionally and with very few goodbyes—we made far more fuss in the old days about a weekend visit

Now that at last it has come—this privileged moment for which I have worked and waited—my heart is very quiet. It's the test of a character which I have often doubted. I shall be glad not to have to doubt it again.

Whatever happens, I know you will be glad to remember

that at a great crisis I tried to play the man, however small my qualifications.

We have always lived so near to one another's affections that this going out alone is more lonely to me than to most men. I have always had someone near at hand with love-blinded eyes to see my faults as springing from higher motives.

Now I reach out my hands across six thousand miles and only touch yours with my imagination to say good bye. What queer sights these eyes, which have been almost your eyes, will witness! If my hands do anything respectable, remember that it is your hands that are doing it. It is your influence as a family that has made me ready for the part I have to play, and where I go, you follow me.

Poor little circle of three loving persons, please be tremendously brave. Don't let anything turn you into cowards—we've all got to be worthy of each other's sacrifice; the greater the sacrifice may prove to be for the one the greater the nobility demanded of the remainder. How idle the words sound, and yet they will take deep meanings when time has given them graver sanctions. I think gallant is the word I've been trying to find—we must be gallant English women and gentlemen.

It's been raining all day and I got very wet this morning. Don't you wish I had caught some quite harmless sickness ? When I didn't want to go back to school, I used to wet my socks purposely in order to catch cold, but the cold always avoided me when I wanted it badly. How far away the childish past seems—almost as though it never happened. And was I really the budding novelist in New York? Life has become so stern and scarlet—and so brave. From my window I look out on the English Channel, a cold, grey-green sea, with rain driving across it and a fleet of small craft taking shelter. Over there beyond the curtain of mist lies France—and everything that awaits me.

News has just come that I have to start. Will continue from France.

Yours ever lovingly,
Con.

7

Friday, September 1st, 1916, 11 a.m.

Dearest Father and Mother:

I embark at 12.30—so this is the last line before I reach France.
I expect the boys are now within sight of English shores—I wish
I could have had an hour with them.

I'm going to do my best to bring you honour—remember
that—I shall do things for your sake out there, living up to the
standards you have taught me.

Yours with a heart full of love,

Con.

8

France, September 1st, 1916.

Dearest M.:

Here I am in France with the same strange smells and street
cries, and almost the same little boys bowling hoops over the
very cobbly cobble stones. I had afternoon tea at a *patisserie* and
ate a great many *gâteaux* for the sake of old times. We had a very
choppy crossing, and you would most certainly have been sick
had you been on board. It seemed to me that I must be coming on one of those romantic holidays to see churches and dead
history—only the khaki-clad figures reminded me that I was
coming to see history in the making.

It's a funny world that batters us about so. It's three years since
I was in France—the last time was with Arthur in Provence. It's
five years since you and I did our famous trip together. I wish
you were here—there are heaps of English nurses in the streets.
I expect to sleep in this place and proceed to my destination
tomorrow.

How I wish I could send you a really descriptive letter! If
I did, I fear you would not get it—so I have to write in gen-
eralities. None of this seems real—it's a kind of wild pretence
from which I shall awake—and when I tell you my dream you'll
laugh and say, "How absurd of you, dreaming that you were a
soldier. I must say you look like it."

Goodbye, my dearest girl,
God bless you,
Con.

9

September 8th, 1916.

My Dearest Ones:

I'm sending this to meet you on your return from Kootenay. I left England on September 1st and had a night at my point of disembarkation, and then set off on a wandering adventure in search of my division. I'm sure you'll understand that I cannot enter into any details—I can only give you general and purely personal impressions. There were two other officers with me, both from Montreal. We had to picnic on chocolate and wine for twenty-four hours through our lack of forethought in not supplying ourselves with food for the trip. I shaved the first morning with water from the exhaust of a railroad engine, having first balanced my mirror on the step.

The engineer was fascinated with my safety razor. There were Tommies from the trenches in another train, muddied to the eyes—who showed themselves much more resourceful. They cooked themselves quite admirable meals as they squatted on the rails, over little fires on which they perched tomato cans. Sunday evening we saw our first German prisoners—a young and degenerate-looking lot. Sunday evening we got off at a station in the rain, and shouldered our own luggage.

Our luggage, by the way, consists of a sleeping bag, in which much of our stuff is packed, and a kit sack—for an immediate change and toilet articles one carries a haversack hung across the shoulder. Well, as I say, we alighted and coaxed a military wagon to come to our rescue. As we set off through a drizzling rain, trudging behind the cart, a double rainbow shone, which I took for an omen. Presently we came to a rest camp, where we told our sad story of empty tummies, and were put up for the night.

A Jock—all Highlanders are called Jock—looked after us. Next morning we started out afresh in a motor lorry and finished at a

Y. M. C. A. tent, where we stayed two nights. On Wednesday we met the general in command of our division, who posted me to the battery, which is said to be the best in the best brigade in the best division—so you may see I'm in luck. I found the battery just having come out of action—we expect to go back again in a day or two. Major B. is the O. C.—a fine man. The lieutenant who shares my tent won the Military Cross at Ypres last Spring. I'm very happy—which will make you happy—and longing for my first taste of real war.

How strangely far away I am from you—all the experiences so unshared and different. Long before this reaches you I shall have been in action several times. This time three years ago my streak of luck came to me and I was prancing round New York. Today I am much more genuinely happy in mind, for I feel, as I never felt when I was only writing, that I am doing something difficult which has no element of self in it. If I come back, life will be a much less restless affair.

This letter! I can imagine it being delivered and the shout from whoever takes it and the comments. I make the contrast in my mind—this little lean-to spread of canvas about four feet high, the horse-lines, guns, sentries going up and down—and then the dear home and the well-loved faces. ,

Goodbye. Don't be at all nervous.

Yours lovingly,

Con.

10

September 12th, Tuesday.

Dearest M.:

You will already have received my first letters giving you my address over here. The wagon has just come up to our position, but it has brought me only one letter since I've been across. I'm sitting in my dugout with shells passing over my head with the sound of ripping linen. I've already had the novel experience of firing a battery, and tomorrow I go up to the first line trenches.

It's extraordinary how commonplace war becomes to a man

who is thrust among others who consider it commonplace. Not fifty yards away from me a dead German lies rotting and uncovered—I daresay he was buried once and then blown out by a shell.

Wednesday, 7 p.m.

Your letters came two hours ago—the first to reach me here—and I have done little else but read and re-read them. How they bring the old ways of life back with their love and longing! Dear mother's tie will be worn tomorrow, and it will be ripping to feel that it was made by her hands. Your cross has not arrived yet, dear. Your mittens will be jolly for the winter. I've heard nothing from the boys yet.

Today I took a trip into No-Man's Land—when the war is ended I'll be able to tell you all about it. I think the picture is photographed upon my memory forever. There's so much you would like to hear and so little I'm allowed to tell. Ask G. M'C. if he was at Princeton with a man named Price—an instructor there.

You ought to see the excitement when the water-cart brings us our mail and the letters are handed out. Some of the gunners have evidently told their Canadian girls that they are officers, and so they are addressed on their letters as lieutenants, I have to censor some of their replies, and I can tell you they are as often funny as pathetic. The ones to their mothers are childish, too, and have rows of kisses. I think men are always kiddies if you look beneath the surface.

The snapshots did fill me with a wanting to be with you in Kootenay. But that's not where you'll receive this. There'll probably be a fire in the sitting-room at home, and a strong aroma of coffee and tobacco. You'll be sitting in a low chair before the fire and your fingers rubbing the hair above your left ear as you read this aloud. I'd like to walk in on you and say, "No more need for letters now." Someday soon, I pray and expect.

Tell dear Papa and Mother that their answers come next. What a lot of love you each one manage to put into your written pages! I'm afraid if I let myself go that way I might make you unhappy.

Since writing this far I have had supper. I'm now sleeping in a new dugout and get a shower of mould on my sleeping-kit each time the guns are fired. One doesn't mind that particularly, especially when you know that the earth walls make you safe. I have a candle in an old petrol tin and dodge the shadows as I write. You know, this artillery game is good sport and one takes everything as it comes with a joke. The men are splendid—their cheeriness comes up bubbling whenever the occasion calls for the dumps. Certainly there are fine qualities which war, despite its unnaturalness, develops. I'm hats off to every infantry private I meet now-a-days.

God bless you and all of you.

Yours lovingly,

Con.

11

September 15th, 1916.

Dear Father:

Your last letter to me was written on a quiet morning in August—in the summer house at Kootenay. It came up yesterday evening on a water-cart from the wagon-lines to a scene a little in contrast.

It's a fortnight today since I left England, and already I've seen action. Things move quickly in this game, and it is a game—one which brings out both the best and the worst qualities in a man. If unconscious heroism is the virtue most to be desired, and heroism spiced with a strong sense of humour at that, then pretty well every man I have met out here has the amazing guts to wear his crown of thorns as though it were a cap-and-bells. To do that for the sake of corporate stout-heartedness is, I think, the acme of what Aristotle meant by virtue.

A strong man, or a good man or a brainless man, can walk to meet pain with a smile on his mouth because he knows that he is strong enough to bear it, or worthy enough to defy it, or because he is such a fool that he has no imagination. But these chaps are neither particularly strong, good, nor brainless; they're more like children, utterly casual with regard to trouble, and quite aware that it is useless to struggle against their elders. So they have the merriest of times while they can, and when the governess, Death, summons them to bed, they obey her with unsurprised quietness.

It sends the mercury of one's optimism rising to see the way they do it I search my mind to find the bigness of motive which supports them, but it forever evades me. These lads are not the kind who philosophise about life; they're the sort, many of them, who would ordinarily wear corduroys and smoke a cutty pipe. I suppose the Christian martyrs would have done the same had corduroys been the fashion in that day, and if a Roman Raleigh had discovered tobacco.

I wrote this about midnight and didn't get any further, as I was up till six carrying on and firing the battery. After adding another page or two I want to get some sleep, as I shall probably have to go up to the observation station to watch the effect of fire tonight. But before I turn in I want to tell you that I had the most gorgeous mail from everybody. Now that I'm in touch with you all again, it's almost like saying "How do?" every night and morning.

I daresay you'll wonder how it feels to be under shell-fire. This is how it feels—you don't realise your danger until you come to think about it afterwards—at the time it's like playing cocoanut shies at a *coon's* head—only you're the *coon's* head. You take too much interest in the sport of dodging to be afraid. You'll hear the Tommies saying if one bursts nearly on them, "Line, you blighter, line. Five minutes more left," just as though they were reprimanding the unseen Hun battery for rotten shooting.

The great word of the Tommies here is "No bloody *bon*"—a strange mixture of French and English, which means that a thing is no good.

If it pleases them it's Jake—though where Jake comes from nobody knows.

Now I must get a wink or two, as I don't know when I may

have to start off.

Ever yours, with love.

Con.

12

September 19th, 1916.

Dearest Mother:

I've been in France nineteen days, and it hasn't taken me long to go into action. Soon I shall be quite an old hand. I'm just back from 24 hours in the observation post, from which one watches the effect of fire. I understand now and forgive the one phrase which the French children have picked up from our Tommies on account of its frequent occurrence—"bl——— mud."

I never knew that mud could be so thick and treacly. All my fear that I might be afraid under shell-fire is over—you get to believe that if you're going to be hit you're going to be. But David's phrase keeps repeating itself in my mind, "*Ten thousand shall fall at thy side, etc., but it shall not come nigh unto thee.*" It's a curious thing that the men who are most afraid are those who get most easily struck.

A friend of G. M'C.'s was hit the other day within thirty yards of me—he was a Princeton chap. I mentioned him in one of my previous letters. Our right section commander got a blighty two days ago and is probably now in England. He went off on a firing battery wagon, grinning all over his face, saying he wouldn't sell that bit of blood and shrapnel for a thousand pounds. I'm wearing your tie—it's the envy of the battery. All the officers wanted me to give them the name of my girl. It never occurs to men that mothers will do things like that.

Thank the powers it has stopped raining and we'll be able to get dry. I came in plastered from head to foot with lying in the rain on my tummy and peering over the top of a trench. Isn't it a funny change from comfortable breakfasts, press notices and a blazing fire?

Do you want any German souvenirs? Just at present I can get plenty. I have a splendid bayonet and a belt with Kaiser Bill's arms on it—but you can't forward these things from France. The Germans swear that they're not using bayonets with saw-edges, but you can buy them for five *francs* from the Tommies—ones they've taken from the prisoners or else picked up.

You needn't be nervous about me. I'm a great little dodger of whizz-bangs. Besides I have a superstition that there's something in the power of M's cross to bless. It came with the mittens, and is at present round my neck.

You know what it sounds like when they're shooting coals down an iron runway into a cellar—well, imagine a thousand of them. That's what I'm hearing while I write.

God bless you; I'm very happy.

Yours ever.

Con.

The reference in the previous letter to a cross is to a little bronze cross of Francis of Assisi.

Many years ago I visited Assisi, and, on leaving, the monks gave me four of these small bronze crosses, assuring me that those who wore them were securely defended in all peril by the efficacious prayers of St. Francis.

Just before Coningsby left Shorncliff to go to France he wrote to us and asked if we couldn't send him something to hang round his neck for luck. We fortunately had one of these crosses of St. Francis at the ranch, and his sister—the M. of these letters— sent it to him. It arrived safely, and he has worn it ever since.

13

September 19th, 1916.

Dearest Father:

I'm writing you your birthday letter early, as I don't know how busy I may be in the next week, nor how long this may take to reach you. You know how much love I send you and how I would like to be with you, D'you remember the birthday three years ago when we set the victrola going outside your room door? Those were my high-jinks days when very many things seemed possible. I'd rather be the person I am now than the person I was then. Life was selfish though glorious.

Well, I've seen my first modern battlefield and am quite disillusioned about the splendour of war. The splendour is all in the souls of the men who creep through the squalor like vermin—it's in nothing external. There was a chap here the other day who deserved the V. C. four times over by running back through the Hun shell fire to bring news that the infantry wanted more artillery support. I was observing for my brigade in the forward station at the time. How he managed to live through the ordeal nobody knows. But men laugh while they do these things. It's fine.

A modern battlefield is the abomination of abominations. Imagine a vast stretch of dead country, pitted with shell-holes as though it had been mutilated with small-pox. There's not a leaf or a blade of grass in sight Every house has either been levelled or is in ruins. No bird sings. Nothing stirs. The only live sound is at night—the scurry of rats. You enter a kind of ditch, called a trench; it leads on to another and another in an unjoyful maze. From the sides feet stick out, and arms and faces—the dead of previous encounters.

"One of our chaps," you say casually, recognising him by his boots or khaki, or "Poor blighter—a, Hun!"

One can afford to forget enmity in the presence of the dead. It is horribly difficult sometimes to distinguish between the living and the slaughtered—they both lie so silently in their little kennels in the earthen bank. You push on—especially if you are doing observation work, till you are past your own front line and out in No Man's Land. You have to crouch and move warily now. Zing! A bullet from a German sniper. You laugh and whisper, "A near one, that."

My first trip to the trenches was up to No Man's Land. I went in the early dawn and came to a Madame Tussaud's show of the dead, frozen into immobility in the most extraordinary attitudes. Some of them were part way out of the ground, one hand pressed to the wound, the other pointing, the head sunken and the hair plastered over the forehead by repeated rains. I kept on wondering what my companions would look like had they been three weeks dead.

My imagination became ingeniously and vividly morbid. When I had to step over them to pass, it seemed as though they must clutch at my trench coat and ask me to help. Poor lonely people, so brave and so anonymous in their death!

Somewhere there is a woman who loved each one of them and would give her life for my opportunity to touch the poor clay that had been kind to her. It's like walking through the day of resurrection to visit No Man's Land. Then the Huns see you and the shrapnel begins to fall—you crouch like a dog and run for it

One gets used to shell-fire up to a point, but there's not a man who doesn't want to duck when he hears one coming. The worst of all is the whizz-bang, because it doesn't give you a chance—it pounces and is on you the same moment that it bangs. There's so much I wish that I could tell you. I can only say this, at the moment we're making history.

What a curious birthday letter! I think of all your other birthdays—the ones before I met these silent men with the green and yellow faces, and the blackened lips which will never speak again. What happy times we have had as a family—what happy jaunts when you took me in those early days, dressed in a sailor suit, when you went hunting pictures. Yet, for all the damnability of what I now witness, I was never quieter in my heart. To have surrendered to an imperative self-denial brings a peace which self-seeking never brought

So don't let this birthday be less gay for my absence. It ought to be the proudest in your life—proud because your example has taught each of your sons to do the difficult things which seem right. It would have been a condemnation of you if any one of us had been a shirker.

I want to buy fine things for you
And be a soldier if I can.

The lines come back to me now. You read them to me first in the dark little study from a green oblong book. You little thought that I would be a soldier—even now I can hardly realise the fact. It seems a dream from which I shall wake up. Am I really killing men day by day? Am I really in jeopardy myself?

Whatever happens I'm not afraid, and I'll give you reason to be glad of me.

Very much love.

Con,

The poem referred to in this letter was actually written for Coningsby when he was between five and six years old. The dark little study which he describes was in the old house at Wesley's Chapel, in the City Road, London—and it was very dark, with only one window, looking out upon a dingy yard. The green oblong book in which I used to write my poems I still have; and it is an illustration of the tenacity of a child's memory that he should recall it. The poem was called A Little Boy's Programme, and ran thus:

I am so very young and small,
That, when big people pass me by,
I sometimes think they are so high
I'll never be a man at all.

And yet I want to be a man
Because so much I want to do;
I want to buy fine things for you
And be a soldier, if I can.

When I'm a man I will not let
Poor little children starve, or be
Ill-used, or stand and beg of me
With naked feet out in the wet

Now, don't you laugh!—The father kissed
The little serious mouth and said
"You've almost made me cry instead.
You blessed little optimist."

14

September 21st, 19161

My Very Dear M.:

I am wearing your talisman while I write and have a strong superstition in its efficacy. The efficacy of your socks is also very noticeable—I wore them the first time on a trip to the Forward Observation Station. I had to lie on my tummy in the mud, my nose just showing above the parapet, for the best part of twenty-four hours. Your socks little thought I would take them into such horrid places when you made them.

Last night both the king and Sir Sam sent us congratulations—I popped in just at the right time. I daresay you know far more about our doings than I do. Only this morning I picked up the *London Times* and read a full account of everything I have witnessed. The account is likely to be still fuller in the New York papers. "Home for Christmas"—that's what the Tommies are promising their mothers and sweethearts in all their letters that I censor. Yesterday I was offered an Imperial commission in the army of occupation. But home for Christmas, will be Christmas, 1917—I can't think that it will be earlier.

Very much love,

Con,

15

Sunday, September 24th, 1916.

Dearest Mother:

Your locket has just reached me, and I have strung it round my neck with M.'s cross. Was it M.'s cross the other night that accounted for my luck? I was in a gun-pit when a shell landed, killing a man only a foot away from me and wounding three others—I and the sergeant were the only two to get out all right. Men who have been out here some time have a dozen stories of similar near squeaks. And talking of squeaks, it was a mouse that saved one man. It kept him awake to such an extent that he determined to move to another place. Just as he got outside the dugout a shell fell on the roof.

You'll be pleased to know that we have a ripping chaplain or *Padre*, as they call chaplains, with us. He plays the game, and I've struck up a great friendship with him. We discuss literature and religion when we're feeling a bit fed up. We talk at home of our faith being tested—one begins to ask strange questions here when he sees what men are allowed by the Almighty to do to one another, and so it's a fine thing to be in constant touch with a great-hearted chap who can risk his life daily to speak of the life hereafter to dying Tommies.

I wish I could tell you of my doings, but it's strictly against orders. You may read in the papers of actions in which I've taken part and never know that I was there.

We live for the most part on tinned stuff, but our appetites make anything taste palatable. Living and sleeping in the open air keeps one ravenous. And one learns to sleep the sleep of the just despite the roaring of the guns.

God bless you each one and give us peaceful hearts.

Yours ever,

Con.

16

September 28th, 1916

My Dears:

We're in the midst of a fine old show, so I don't get much opportunity for writing. Suffice it to say that I've seen the big side of war by now and the extraordinary uncalculating courage of it. Men run out of a trench to an attack with as much eagerness as they would display in overtaking a late bus. If you want to get an idea of what meals are like when a row is on, order the McAlpin to spread you a table where 34th crosses Broadway—and wait for the uptown traffic on the elevated. It's wonderful to see the waiters dodging with dishes through the shell-holes.

It's a wonderful autumn day, golden and mellow; I picture to myself what this country must have looked like before the desolation of war struck it.

I was brigade observation officer on September 26th, and

wouldn't have missed what I saw for a thousand dollars. It was a touch and go business, with shells falling everywhere and machine-gun fire—but something glorious to remember. I had the great joy of being useful in setting a Hun position on fire. I think the war will be over in a twelvemonth.

Our great joy is composing menus of the meals we'll eat when we get home. Goodbye for the present.

Con,

17

October 1st, 1916.

My Dearest M.:

Sunday morning, your first back in Newark. You're not up yet owing to the difference in time—I can imagine the quiet house with the first of the morning stealing greyly in. You'll be presently going to church to sit in your old-fashioned mahogany pew. There's not much of Sunday in our atmosphere—only the little one can manage to keep in his heart. I shall share the echo of yours by remembering.

I'm waiting orders at the present moment to go forward with the colonel and pick out a new gun position. You know I'm very happy—satisfied for the first time I'm doing something big enough to make me forget all failures and self-contempts. I know at last that I can measure up to the standard I have always coveted for myself. So don't worry yourselves about any note of hardship that you may interpret into my letters, for the deprivation is fully compensated for by the winged sense of exaltation one has.

Things have been a little warm round us lately. A gun to our right, another to our rear and another to our front were knocked out with direct hits. We've got some of the chaps taking their meals with us now because their mess was all shot to blazes. There was an officer who was with me at the 53rd blown thirty feet into the air while I was watching. He picked himself up and insisted on carrying on, although his face was a mass of bruises. I walked in on the biggest engagement of the entire war

43

the moment I came out here. There was no gradual breaking-in for me. My first trip to the front line was into a trench full of dead.

Have you seen Lloyd George's great speech? I'm all with him. No matter what the cost and how many of us have to give our lives, this war must be so finished that war may be forever at an end. If the devils who plan wars could only see the abysmal result of their handiwork!

Give them one day in the trenches under shell-fire when their lives aren't worth a five minutes' purchase—or one day carrying back the wounded through this tortured country, or one day in a Red Cross train. No one can imagine the damnable waste and Christlessness of this battering of human flesh. The only way that this war can be made holy is by making it so thorough that war will be finished for all time.

Papa at least will be awake by now. How familiar the old house seems to me—I can think of the place of every picture. Do you set the victrola going now-a-days? I bet you play *Boys in Khaki, Boys in Blue*.

Please send me anything in the way of eatables that the goodness of your hearts can imagine—also smokes.

Later.

I came back from the front-line all right and have since been hard at it firing. Your letters reached me in the midst of a bombardment—I read them in a kind of London fog of gunpowder smoke, with my steel helmet tilted back, in the interval of commanding my section through a megaphone.

Don't suppose that I'm in any way unhappy—I'm as cheerful as a cricket and do twice as much hopping—I have to. There's something extraordinarily bracing about taking risks and getting away with it—especially when you know that you're contributing your share to a far-reaching result.

My mother is the mother of a soldier now, and soldiers' mothers don't lie awake at night imagining—they just say a prayer for their sons and leave everything in God's hands. I'm sure you'd far rather I died than not play the man to the fullest

44

of my strength.

It isn't when you die that matters—it's how. Not but what I intend to return to Newark and make the house reek of tobacco smoke before I've done.

We're continually in action now, and the casualty to B. has left us short-handed—moreover we're helping out another battery which has lost two officers. As you've seen by the papers, we've at last got the Hun on the run. Three hundred passed me the other day unescorted, coming in to give themselves up as prisoners. They're the dirtiest lot you ever set eyes on, and looked as though they hadn't eaten for months.

I wish I could send you some souvenirs. But we can't send them out of France.

I'm scribbling by candlelight and everything's jumping with the stamping of the guns. I wear the locket and cross all the time.

Yours with much love,
Con.

18

October 13th, 1916

Dear Ones:

I have only time to write and assure you that I am safe. We're living in trenches at present—I have my sleeping bag placed on a stretcher to keep it fairly dry. By the time you get this we expect to be having a rest, as we've been hard at it now for an unusually long time. How I wish that I could tell you so many things that are big and vivid in my mind—but the censor—!

Yesterday I had an exciting day. I was up forward when word came through that an officer still further forward was wounded and he'd been caught in a heavy enemy fire. I had only a kid telephonist with me, but we found a stretcher, went forward and got him out.

The earth was hopping up and down like popcorn in a frying pan. The unfortunate thing was that the poor chap died on the way out. It was only the evening before that we had dined together and he had told me what he was going to do with his next leave.

God bless you all,
Con.

19

October 14th, 1916.

Dearest Mother:

I'm still all right and well. Today I had the funniest experience of my life—got caught in a Hun curtain of fire and had to lie on my tummy for two hours in a trench with the shells bursting five yards from me—and never a scratch. You know how I used to wonder what I'd do under such circumstances. Well, I laughed. All I could think of was the sleek people walking down Fifth Avenue, and the equally sleek crowds taking tea at the Waldorf. It struck me as ludicrous that I, who had been one of them, should be lying there lunchless. For a little while I was slightly deaf with the concussions. That poem keeps on going through my head,

Oh, to come home once more, when the dusk is falling,
To see the nursery lighted and the children's table spread;
"Mother, mother, mother!" the eager voices calling,
"The baby was so sleepy that he had to go to bed!"

Wouldn't it be good, instead of sitting in a Hun dugout?
Yours lovingly,
Con.

20

October 15th, 1916

Dear Ones:

We're still in action, but are in hopes that soon we may be moved to winter quarters. We've had our taste of mud, and are anxious to move into better quarters before we get our next. I think I told you that our O. C. had got wounded in the feet,

46

and our right section commander got it in the shoulder a little earlier—so we're a bit short-handed and find ourselves with plenty of work.

I have curiously lucid moments when recent happenings focus themselves in what seems to be their true perspective. The other night I was forward observation officer on one of our recent battlefields. I had to watch the front all night for signals, etc. There was a full white moon sailing serenely overhead, and when I looked at it I could almost fancy myself back in the old melancholy pomp of autumn woodlands where the leaves were red, not with the colour of men's blood.

My mind went back to so many bygone days—especially to three years ago. I seemed so vastly young then, upon reflection. For a little while I was full of regrets for many things wasted, and then I looked at the battlefield with its scattered kits and broken rifles. Nothing seemed to matter very much.

A rat came out—then other rats. I stood there feeling extraordinarily aloof from all things that can hurt, and—you'll smile—I planned a novel. O, if I get back, how differently I shall write! When you've faced the worst in so many forms, you lose your fear and arrive at peace. There's a marvellous grandeur about all this carnage and desolation—men's souls rise above the distress—they have to in order to survive. When you see how cheap men's bodies are you cannot help but know that the body is the least part of personality.

You can let up on your nervousness when you get this, for I shall almost certainly be in a safer zone. We've done more than our share and must be withdrawn soon. There's hardly a battery which does not deserve a dozen D. S. O.'s with a V. C. or two thrown in.

It's 4.30 now—you'll be in church and, I hope, wearing my flowers. Wait till I come back and you shall go to church with the biggest bunch of roses that ever were pinned to a feminine chest. I wonder when that will be.

We have heaps of humour out here. You should have seen me this morning, sitting on the gun-seat while my batman cut my hair.

A sandbag was spread over my shoulders in place of a towel and the gun-detachment stood round and gave advice. I don't know what I look like, for I haven't dared to gaze into my shaving mirror.

Good luck to us all.

Con.

21

October 18th, 1916.

Dearest M.:

I've come down to the lines today; tomorrow I go back again. I'm sitting alone in a deep chalk dugout—it is 10 p.m. and I have lit a fire by splitting wood with a bayonet. Your letters from Montreal reached me yesterday. They came up in the water-cart when we'd all begun to despair of mail.

It was wonderful the silence that followed while everyone went back home for a little while, and most of them met their best girls.

We've fallen into the habit of singing in parts. *Jerusalem the Golden* is a great favourite as we wait for our breakfast—we go through all our favourite songs, including *Poor Old Adam Was My Father*.

Our greatest favourite is one which is symbolising the hopes that are in so many hearts on this greatest battlefield in history. We sing it under shell-fire as a kind of prayer, we sing it as we struggle knee-deep in the appalling mud, we sing it as we sit by a candle in our deep captured German dugouts. It runs like this:

There's a long, long trail a-winding
Into the land of my dreams,
Where the nightingales are singing
And a white moon beams:

There's a long, long night of waiting
Until my dreams all come true;
Till the day when I'll be going down
That long, long trail with you.

You ought to be able to get it, and then you will be singing

48

it when I'm doing it.

No, I don't know what to ask from you for Christmas—unless a plum pudding and a general surprise box of sweets and food stuffs. If you don't mind my suggesting it, I wouldn't a bit mind a Christmas box at once—schoolboy's tuck box. I wear the locket, cross, and tie all the time as kind of charms against danger—they give me the feeling of loving hands going with me everywhere.

God bless you.

Yours ever,

Con.

22

October 23rd, 1916.

Dearest All:

As you know I have been in action ever since I left England and am still. I've lived in various extemporised dwellings and am at present writing from an eight foot deep hole dug in the ground and covered over with galvanised iron and sandbags. We have made ourselves very comfortable, and a fire is burning—I correct that—comfortable until it rains, I should say, when the water finds its own level. We have just finished with two days of penetrating rain and mist—in the trenches the mud was up to my knees, so you can imagine the joy of wading down these shell-torn tunnels. Good thick socks have been priceless.

You'll be pleased to hear that two days ago I was made Right Section Commander—which is fairly rapid promotion. It means a good deal more work and responsibility, but it gives me a contact with the men which I like.

I don't know when I'll get leave—not for another two months anyway. It would be ripping if I had word in time for you to run over to England for the brief nine days.

I plan novels galore and wonder whether I shall ever write them the way I see them now. My imagination is to an extent crushed by the stupendousness of reality. I think I am changed in some stern spiritual way—stripped of flabbiness. I am perhaps harder—I can't say.

That I should be a novelist seems unreasonable—it's so long since I had my own way in the world and met anyone on artistic terms. But I have enough ego left to be very interested in my book. And by the way, when we're out at the front and the battery wants ns to come in they simply phone up the password, "Slaves of Freedom," the meaning of which we all understand.

You are ever in my thoughts, and I pray the day may not be far distant when we meet again.

Con.

23

October 27th, 1916.

Dearest Family:

All today I've been busy registering our guns. There is little chance of rest—one would suppose that we intended to end the war by spring.

Two new officers joined our battery from England, which makes the work lighter. One of them brings the news that D., one of the two officers who crossed over from England with me and wandered through France with me in search of our division, is already dead. He was a corking fellow, and I'm very sorry. He was caught by a shell in the head and legs.

I am still living in a sandbagged shell-hole eight feet beneath the level of the ground. I have a sleeping bag with an eiderdown inside it, for my bed; it is laid on a stretcher, which is placed in a roofed-in trench. For meals, when there isn't a block on the roads, we do very well; we subscribe pretty heavily to the mess, and have an officer back at the wagon-lines to do our purchasing.

When we move forward into a new position, however, we go pretty short, as roads have to be built for the throng of traffic. Most of what we eat is tinned—and I never want to see tinned salmon again when this war is ended. I have a personal servant, a groom and two horses—but haven't been on a horse for seven weeks on account of being in action. We're all pretty fed up with continuous firing and living so many hours in the trenches.

The way artillery is run today an artillery lieutenant is more in the trenches than an infantryman—the only thing he doesn't do is to go over the parapet in an attack. And one of our chaps did that the other day, charging the Huns with a bar of chocolate in one hand and a revolver in the other. I believe he set a fashion which will be imitated. Three times in my experience I have seen the infantry jump out of their trenches and go across. It's a sight never to be forgotten.

One time there were machine guns behind me and they sent a message to me, asking me to lie down and take cover. That was impossible, as I was observing for my brigade, so I lay on the parapet till the bullets began to fall too close for comfort, then I dodged out into a shell-hole with the German barrage bursting all around me, and had a most gorgeous view of a modern attack. That was some time ago, so you needn't be nervous.

Have I mentioned rum to you? I never tasted it to my knowledge until I came out here. We get it served us whenever we're wet. It's the one thing which keeps a man alive in the winter—you can sleep when you're drenched through and never get a cold if you take it.

At night, by a fire, eight feet underground, we sing all the dear old songs. We manage a kind of glee—*Clementina, The Long, Long Trail, Three Blind Mice, Long, Long Ago, Rock of Ages.* Hymns are quite favourites.

Don't worry about me; your prayers weave round me a mantle of defence.

Yours with more love than I can write,
Con.

24

October 31st, 1916.
Hallowe'en.
Dearest People;
Once more I'm taking the night-firing and so have a chance to write to you. I got letters from you all, and they each de-

serve answers, but I have so little time to write. We've been having beastly weather—drowned out of our little houses below ground, with rivers running through our beds. The mud is once more up to our knees and gets into whatever we eat. The wonder is that we keep healthy—I suppose it's the open air. My throat never troubles me and I'm free from colds in spite of wet feet. The main disadvantage is that we rarely get a chance to wash or change our clothes. Your ideas of an army with its buttons all shining is quite erroneous; we look like drunk and disorderlies who have spent the night in the gutter—and we have the same instinct for fighting.

In the trenches the other day I heard mother's Suffolk tongue and had a jolly talk with a chap who shared many of my memories. It was his first trip in and the Huns were shelling badly, but he didn't seem at all upset.

We're still hard at it and have given up all idea of a rest—the only way we'll get one is with a blighty. You say how often you tell yourselves that the same moon looks down on me; it does, but on a scene how different! We advance over old battlefields—everything is blasted. If you start digging, you turn up what's left of something human. If there were any grounds for superstition, surely the places in which I have been should be ghost-haunted. One never thinks about it. For myself I have increasingly the feeling that I am protected by your prayers; I tell myself so when I am in danger.

Here I sit in an old sweater and muddy breeches, the very reverse of your picture of a soldier, and I imagine to myself your receipt of this. Our chief interest is to enquire whether milk, jam and mail have come up from the wagon-lines; it seems a faery-tale that there are places where milk and jam can be had for the buying. See how simple we become.

Poor little house at Kootenay! I hate to think of it empty. We had such good times there twelve months ago. They have a song here to a nursery rhyme lilt, Après le Guerre Finis; it goes on to tell of all the good times we'll have when the war is ended. Every night I invent a new story of my own celebration of the event, usually, as when I was a kiddie, just before I fall asleep—only it doesn't seem possible that the war will ever end.

I hear from the boys very regularly. There's just the chance that I may get leave to London in the New Year and meet them before they set out. I always picture you with your heads high in the air. I'm glad to think of you as proud because of the pain we've made you suffer.

Once again I shall think of you on Papa's birthday. I don't think this will be the saddest he will have to remember. It might have been if we three boys had still all been with him. If I were a father, I would prefer at all costs that my sons should be men. What good comrades we've always been, and what long years of happy times we have in memory—all the way down from a little boy in a sailor-suit to Kootenay!

I fell asleep in the midst of this. I've now got to go out and start the other gun firing. With very much love.

Yours,

Con.

25

November 1st, 1916.

My Dearest M.:

Peace after a storm! Your letter was not brought up by the water-wagon this evening, but by an orderly—the mud prevented wheel-traffic. I was just sitting down to read it when Fritz began to pay us too much attention. I put down your letter, grabbed my steel helmet, rushed out to see where the shells were falling, and then cleared my men to a safer area. (By the way, did I tell you that I had been made Right Section Commander?)

After about half an hour I came back and settled down by a fire made of smashed ammunition boxes in a stove borrowed from a ruined cottage. I'm always ashamed that my letters contain so little news and are so uninteresting. This thing is so big and dreadful that it does not bear putting down on paper.

I read the papers with the accounts of singing soldiers and other rubbish; they depict us as though we were a lot of hair-brained idiots instead of men fully realising our danger, who plod on because it's our duty. I've seen a good many men killed by now—we all have—consequently the singing soldier story makes us smile. We've got a big job; we know that we've got to "Carry On" whatever happens—so we wear a stern grin and go to it. There's far more heroism in the attitude of men out here than in the footlight attitude that journalists paint for the public. It isn't a singing matter to go on firing a gun when gun-pits are going up in smoke within sight of you.

What a terrible desecration war is! You go out one week and look through your glasses at a green, smiling country—little churches, villages nestling among woods, white roads running across a green carpet; next week you see nothing but ruins and a country-side pitted with shell-holes.

All night the machine guns tap like rivetting machines when a New York sky-scraper is in the building. Then suddenly in the night a bombing attack will start, and the sky grows white with signal rockets. Orders come in for artillery retaliation, and your guns begin to stamp the ground like stallions; in the darkness on every side you can see them snorting fire. Then stillness again, while Death counts his harvest; the white rockets grow fainter and less hysterical. For an hour there is blackness.

My batman consoles himself with singing,

Pack up your troubles in your old kit-bag,
And smile, smile, smile.

There's a lot in his philosophy—it's best to go on smiling even when someone who was once your pal lies forever silent in his blanket on a stretcher.

The great uplifting thought is that we have proved ourselves men. In our death we set a standard which in ordinary life we could never have followed. Inevitably we should have sunk below our highest self. Here we know that the world will remember us and that our loved ones, in spite of tears, will be proud of us.

What God will say to us we cannot guess—but He can't be

too hard on men who did their duty. I think we all feel that trivial former failures are washed out by this final sacrifice. When little M. used to recite "*Breathes there a man with soul so dead who never to himself had said, 'This is my own, my native land.'*"

I never thought that I should have the chance that has now been given to me. I feel a great and solemn gratitude that I have been thought worthy. Life has suddenly become effective and worthy by reason of its carelessness of death.

By the way, that Princeton man I mentioned so long ago was killed forty yards away from me on my first trip into the trenches. Probably G. M'C. and his other friends know by now. He was the first man I ever saw snuffed out.

I'm wearing your mittens and find them a great comfort, I'll look forward to some more of your socks—I can do with plenty of them. If any of your friends are making things for soldiers, I wish you'd get them to send them to this battery, as they would be gratefully accepted by the men.

I wish I could come to *The Music Master* with you. I wonder how long till we do all those intimately family things together again.

Goodbye, my dearest M. I live for home letters and am rarely disappointed.

God bless you, and love to you all.

Yours ever,

Con.

26

November 4th, 1916.

My Dearest Mother:

This morning I was wakened up in the gun-pit where I was sleeping by the arrival of the most wonderful parcel of mail. It was really a kind of Christmas morning for me. My servant had lit a fire in a punctured petrol can and the place looked very cheery. First of all entered an enormous affair, which turned out to be a stove which C. had sent.

Then there was a sandbag containing all your gifts. You may

bet I made for that first, and as each knot was undone remembered the loving hands that had done it up. I am now going up to a twenty-four-hour shift of observing, and shall take up the malted milk and some blocks of chocolate for a hot drink. It somehow makes you seem very near to me to receive things packed with your hands. When I go forward I shall also take candles and a copy of *Anne Veronica* with me, so that if I get a chance I can forget time.

Always when I write to you odds and ends come to mind, smacking of local colour. After an attack some months ago I met a solitary private wandering across a shell-torn field. I watched him and thought something was wrong by the aimlessness of his progress. When I spoke to him, he looked at me mistily and said, "Dead men. Moonlit road." He kept on repeating the phrase, and it was all that one could get out of him. Probably the dead men and the moonlit road were the last sights he had seen before he went insane.

Another touching thing happened two days ago. A major turned up who had travelled fifty miles by motor lorries and any conveyance he could pick up on the road. He had left his unit to come to have a glimpse of our front-line trench where his son was buried. The boy had died there some days ago in going over the parapet. I persuaded him that he ought not to go alone, and that in any case it wasn't a healthy spot.

At last he consented to let me take him to a point from which he could see the ground over which his son had attacked and led his men. The sun was sinking behind us. He stood there very straightly, peering through my glasses—and then forgot all about me and began speaking to his son in childish love-words. "Gone West," they call dying out here—we rarely say that a man is dead. I found out afterwards that it was the boy's mother the major was thinking of when he pledged himself to visit the grave in the front-line.

But there are happier things than that. For instance, you should hear us singing at night in our dugout—every tune we ever learnt, I believe. *Silver Threads Among the Gold, In the Gloam-*

ing, The Star of Bethlehem, I Hear You Calling Me, interspersed with Everybody Works but Father, and Poor Old Adam, etc.

I wish I could know in time when I get my leave for you to come over and meet me. I'm going to spend my nine days in the most glorious ways imaginable. To start with I won't eat anything that's canned and, to go on, I won't get out of bed till I feel inclined. And if you're there—!

Dreams and nonsense! God bless you all and keep us near and safe though absent. Alive or "Gone West" I shall never be far from you; you may depend on that—and I shall always hope to feel you brave and happy. This is a great game—cheese-mites pitting themselves against all the splendours of Death. Please, please write well ahead, so that I may not miss your Christmas letters,

Yours lovingly.
Con.

27

November 6th, 1916.

My Dear Ones:

Such a wonderful day it has been—I scarcely know where to start. I came down last night from twenty-four hours in the mud, where I had been observing. I'd spent the night in a hole dug in the side of the trench and a dead Hun forming part of the roof. I'd sat there reliving so many things—the ecstatic moments of my life when I first touched fame—and my feet were so cold that I could not feel them, so I thought all the harder of the pleasant things of the past.

Then, as I say, I came back to the gun position to learn that I was to have one day off at the back of the lines. You can't imagine what that meant to me—one day in a country that is green, one day where there is no shell-fire, one day where you don't turn up corpses with your tread! For two months I have never left the guns except to go forward and I have never been from under shell-fire.

All night long as I have slept the ground had been shaken by the stamping of the guns—and now after two months, to come back to comparative normality! The reason for this privilege being granted was that the powers that be had come to the conclusion that it was time I had a bath. Since I sleep in my clothes and water is too valuable for washing anything but the face and hands, they were probably right in their guess at my condition.

So with the greatest holiday of my life in prospect I went to the empty gun-pit in which I sleep, and turned in. This morning I set out early with my servant, tramping back across the long, long battlefields which our boys have won. The mud was knee-deep in places, but we floundered on till we came to our old and deserted gun-position where my horses waited for me. From there I rode to the wagon-lines—the first time I've sat a horse since I came into action. Far behind me the thunder of winged murder grew more faint. The country became greener; trees even had leaves upon them which fluttered against the grey-blue sky. It was wonderful—like awaking from an appalling nightmare. My little beast was fresh and seemed to share my joy, for she stepped out bravely.

When I arrived at the wagon-lines I would not wait—I longed to see something even greener and quieter. My groom packed up some oats and away we went again. My first objective was the military baths; I lay in hot water for half-an-hour and read the advertisements of my book.

As I lay there, for the first time since I've out, I began to get a half-way true perspective of myself. What's left of the egotism of the author came to life, and—now laugh—I planned my next novel—planned it to the sound of men singing, because they were clean for the first time in months. I left my towels and soap with a military policeman, by the roadside, and went prancing off along country roads in search of the almost forgotten places where people don't kill one another.

Was it imagination? There seemed to me to be a different look in the faces of the men I met—for the time being they were neither hunters nor hunted. There were actually cows in the fields. At one point, where pollarded trees stand like a Hobbema sketch against the sky, a group of officers were coursing a hare, following a big black hound on horseback. We lost our way. A drenching rainstorm fell over us—we didn't care; and we saw as we looked back a most beautiful thing—a rainbow over green fields. It was as romantic as the first rainbow in childhood.

All day I have been seeing lovely and familiar things as though for the first time. I've been a sort of Lazarus, rising out of his tomb and praising God at the sound of a divine voice. You don't know how exquisite a ploughed field can look, especially after rain, unless you have feared that you might never see one again.

I came to a grey little village, where civilians were still living, and then to a gate and a garden. In the cottage was a French peasant woman who smiled, patted my hair because it was curly, and chattered interminably. The result was a huge omelette and a bottle of champagne. Then came a touch of naughtiness—a lady visitor with a copy of *La Vie Parisienne*, which she promptly bestowed on the English soldier.

I read it, and dreamt of the time when I should walk the Champs Elysees again. It was growing dusk when I turned back to the noise of battle. There was a white moon in a milky sky. Motorbikes fled by me, great lorries driven by Jehus from London buses, and automobiles which too poignantly had been Strand taxis and had taken lovers home from the Gaiety. I jogged along thinking very little, but supremely happy. Now I'm back at the wagon-line; tomorrow I go back to the guns. Meanwhile I write to you by a guttering candle.

Life, how I love you! What a wonderful kindly thing I could make of you tonight. Strangely the vision has come to me of all that you mean. Now I could write. So soon you may go from me or be changed into a form of existence which all my training has taught me to dread. After death is there only nothingness? I think that for those who have missed love in this life there must be compensations—the little children whom they ought to have had, perhaps. Today, after so many weeks, I have seen little children again.

And yet, so strange a havoc does this war work that, if I have to "Go West," I shall go proudly and quietly. I have seen too many men die bravely to make a fuss if my turn comes. A mixed passenger list old Father Charon must have each night—Englishmen, Frenchmen, and Huns. Tomorrow I shall have another sight of the greenness and then—the guns.

I don't know whether I have been able to make any of my emotions clear to you in my letters. Terror has a terrible fascination. Up to now I have always been afraid—afraid of small fears. At last I meet fear itself and it stings my pride into an unpremeditated courage.

I've just had a pile of letters from you all. How ripping it is to be remembered! Letters keep one civilised.

It's late and I'm very tired. God bless you each and all.

Con.

28

November 15th, 1916.

Dear Father:

I've owed you a letter for some time, but I've been getting very little leisure. You can't send steel messages to the Kaiser and love-notes to your family in the same breath.

I am amazed at the spirit you three are showing and almighty proud that you can muster such courage. I suppose none of us quite realised our strength till it came to the test There was a time when we all doubted our own heroism. I think we were typical of our age. Every novel of the past ten years has been more or less a study in sentiment and self-distrust. We used to wonder what kind of stuff Drake's men were made of that they could jest while they died. We used to contrast ourselves with them to our own disfavour. Well, we know now that when there's a New World to be discovered we can still rise up reincarnated into spiritual pirates.

It wasn't the men of our age who were at fault, but the New World that was lacking. Our New World is the Kingdom of Heroism, the doors of which are flung so wide that the meanest of us may enter. I know men out here who are the dependable daredevils of their brigades, who in peace times were nuisances and as soon as peace is declared will become nuisances again. At the moment they're fine, laughing at Death and smiling at the chance of agony.

There's a man I know of who had a record sheet of crimes. When he was out of action he was always drunk and up for office. To get rid of him, they put him into the trench mortars and within a month he had won his D. C. M. He came out and went on the spree—this particular spree consisted in stripping a Highland officer of his kilts on a moonlight night. For this he was sentenced to several months in a military prison, but asked to be allowed to serve his sentence in the trenches.

He came out from his punishment a King's sergeant—which means that whatever he did nobody could degrade him. He got this for lifting his trench mortar over the parapet when all the detachment were killed. Carrying it out into a shell-hole, he held back the Hun attack and saved the situation. He got drunk again, and again chose to be returned to the trenches. This time his head was blown off while he was engaged in a special feat of gallantry.

What are you to say to such men? Ordinarily they'd be black-guards, but war lifts them into splendour. In the same way you see mild men, timid men, almost girlish men, carrying out duties which in other wars would have won V. C.'s. I don't think the soul of courage ever dies out of the race any more than the capacity for love. All it means is that the occasion is not present. For myself I try to analyse my emotions; am I simply numb, or do I imitate other people's coolness and shall I fear life again when the war is ended? There is no explanation save the great army phrase "Carry on." We "carry on" because, if we don't, we shall let other men down and put their lives in danger. And there's more than that—we all want to live up to the standard that prompted us to come.

One talks about splendour—but war isn't splendid except in the individual sense. A man by his own self-conquest can make it splendid for himself, but in the massed sense it's squalid. There's

nothing splendid about a battlefield when the fight is ended—
shreds of what once were men, tortured, levelled landscapes—
the barbaric loneliness of Hell.

I shall never forget my first dead man. He was a signalling officer, lying in the dawn on a muddy hill. I thought he was asleep
at first, but when I looked more closely, I saw that his shoulder
blade was showing white through his tunic. He was wearing
black boots. It's odd, but the sight of black boots have the same
effect on me now that black and white stripes had in childhood.
I have the superstitious feeling that to wear them would bring
me bad luck.

Tonight we've been singing in parts, *Back in the Dear Dead
Days Beyond Recall*—a mournful kind of ditty to sing under the
circumstances—so mournful that we had to have a game of five
hundred to cheer us up.

It's now nearly 2 a.m., and I have to go out to the guns again
before I go to bed. I carry your letters about in my pockets and
read them at odd intervals in all kinds of places that you can't
imagine.

Cheer up and remember that I'm quite happy. I wish you
could be with me for just one day to understand.

Yours,
Con.

29

December 3rd, 1916.

Dear Boys:

By this time you will be all through your exams and I hope
have both passed. It'll be splendid if you can go together to the
same station. You envy me, you say; well, I rather envy you. I'd
like to be with you.

You, at least, don't have Napoleon's fourth antagonist with
which to contend—mud. But at present I'm clean and billeted
in an estaminet, in a not too bad little village. There's an old
mill and still older church, and the usual farmhouses with the
indispensable pile of manure under the front windows. We shall

have plenty of hard work here, licking our men into shape and refitting.

You know how I've longed to sleep between sheets; I can now, but find them so cold that I still use my sleeping bag—such is human inconsistency. But yesterday I had a boiling bath—as good a bath as could be found in a New York hotel—and I am clean.

I woke up this morning to hear someone singing *Casey Jones*—consequently I thought of former Christmases. My mind has been travelling back very much of late. Suddenly I see something here which reminds me of the time when E. and I were at Lisieux, or even of our Saturday excursions to Nelson when we were all together at the ranch.

Did I tell you that B., our officer who was wounded two months ago, has just returned to us. This morning he got news that his young brother has been killed in the place which we have left. I wonder when we shall grow tired of stabbing and shooting and killing. It seems to me that the war cannot end in less than two years.

I have made myself nice to the brigade interpreter and he has found me a delightful room with electric light and a fire. It's in an old farmhouse with a brick terrace in front. My room is on the ground floor and tile-paved. The chairs are rush-bottomed and there are old quaint china plates on the shelves. There is also a quite charming *mademoiselle*. So you see, you don't need to pity me anymore.

Just at present I'm busy getting up the brigade Christmas entertainment. The Colonel asked me to do it, otherwise I should have said no, as I want all the time I can get to myself. You can't think how jolly it is to sit again in a room which is temporarily yours after living in dugouts, herded side by side with other men. I can be me now, and not a soldier of thousands when I write. You shall hear from me again soon. Hope you're having a ripping time in London.

Yours ever,
Con.

30

December 5th, 1916.

Dearest M.:

I've just come in from my last tour of inspection as orderly officer, and it's close on midnight. I'm getting this line off to you to let you know that I expect to get my nine days' leave about the beginning of January. How I wish it were possible to have you in London when I arrive, or, failing that, to spend my leave in New York!

Tomorrow I make an early start on horseback for a market of the old-fashioned sort which is held at a town nearby. Can you dimly picture me with my groom, followed by a mess-cart, going from stall to stall and bartering with the peasants? It'll be rather good fun and something quite out of my experience.

Christmas will be over by the time you get this, and I do hope that you had a good one. I paused to talk to the other officers; they say that they are sure that you are very beautiful and have a warm heart, and would like to send them a five-storey layer cake, half a dozen bottles of port and one Paris chef. At present I am the Dives of the mess and dole out luxuries to these Lazaruses.

Goodbye for the present.

Yours ever lovingly,

Con.

31

December 6th, 1916.

Dearest M.:

I've just undone your Christmas parcels, and already I am wearing the waistcoat and socks, and my mouth is hot with the ginger.

I expect to get leave for England on January 10th. I do wish it might be possible for some of you to cross the ocean and be in London with me—and I don't see what there is to prevent you. Unless the war ends sooner than any of us expect, it is not likely that I shall get another leave in less than nine months. So, if you want to come and if there's time when you receive this letter, just hop on a boat and let's see what London looks like together.

I wonder what kind of a Christmas you'll have. I shall picture it all. You may hear me tiptoeing up the stairs if you listen very hard. Where does the soul go in sleep? Surely mine flies back to where all of you dear people are.

I came back to my farm yesterday to find a bouquet of paper flowers at the head of my bed with a note pinned on it. Over my fire-place was hung a pathetic pair of farm-girls' heavy Sunday boots, all brightly polished, with two other notes pinned on them. The Feast of St. Nicholas on December 7th is an opportunity for unmarried men to be reminded that there are unmarried girls in the world—wherefore the flowers. I enclose the notes. Keep them,—they may be useful for a book some day.

I'm having a pretty good rest, and am still in my old farm-house.

Love to all.

Con.

32

December 15th, 1916.

Dearest All:

At the present I'm just where mother hoped I'd be—in a deep dugout about twenty feet down—we're trying to get a fire lighted, and consequently the place is smoked out. Where I'll be for Christmas I don't know, but I hope by then to be in billets. I've just come back from the trenches, where I've been observing.

The mud is not nearly so bad where I am now, and with a few days' more work, we should be quite comfortable. You'll have received my cable about my getting leave soon—I'm wondering whether the Atlantic is sufficiently quiet for any of you to risk a crossing.

Poor Basil! Your letter was the first news I got of his death. I must have watched the attack in which he lost his life. One wonders now how it was that some instinct did not warn me that one of those khaki dots jumping out of the trenches was the cousin who stayed with us in London.

I'm wondering what this mystery of the German chancellor is all about—some peace proposals, I suppose—which are sure to prove bombastic and unacceptable. It seems to us out here as though the war must go on forever. Like a boy's dream of the far-off freedom of manhood, the day appears when we shall step out into the old liberty of owning our own lives. What a celebration we'll have when I come home! I can't quite grasp the joy of it.

I've got to get this letter off quite soon if it's to go today. It ought to reach you by January 12th or thereabouts. You may be sure my thoughts will have been with you on Christmas day. I shall look back and remember all the bygone good times and then plan for Christmas, 1917. God keep us all.

Ever yours,
Con.

33

December 18th, 1916.

My Dearest M.:

I always feel when I write a joint letter to the family that I'm cheating each one of you, but it's so very difficult to get time to write as often as I'd like. It's a week to Christmas and I picture the beginnings of the preparations. I can look back and remember so many such preparations, especially when we were kiddies in London.

What good times one has in a life I I've been sitting with my groom by the fire to night while he dried my clothes. I've mentioned him to you before as having lived in Nelson, and worked at the Silver King mine. We both grew ecstatic over British Columbia.

I am hoping all the time that the boys may be in England at the time I get my leave—I hardly dare hope that any of you will be there. But it would be grand if you could manage it—I long very much to see you all again. I can just imagine my first month home again. I shan't let any of you work. I shall be the incurable boy. I've spent the best part of today out in No Man's Land, within seventy yards of the Huns.

Quite an experience, I assure you, and one that I wouldn't have missed for worlds. I'll have heaps to write into novels one day—the vividest kind of local colour. Just at present I have nothing to read but the Christmas number of the *Strand*. It makes me remember the time when we children raced for the latest development of *The Hound of the Baskervilles*, and so many occasions when I had one of "those sniffy colds" and sat by the Highbury fire with a book. Good days, those!

I'm just off to bed now, and will finish this tomorrow. Bed is my greatest luxury nowadays.

December 19th.

The book and chocolate just came, and a bunch, of New York papers. All were most welcome. I was longing for something to read. Tomorrow I have to go forward to observe. Two of our officers are on leave, so it makes the rest of us work pretty hard. What do you think of the *Kaiser's* absurd peace proposals? The man must be mad.

The best of love,
Con.

34

December 20th, 1916.

Dear Mr. T.:

Just back from a successful argument with Fritz, to find your kind good wishes. It's rather a lark out here, though a lark which may turn against you any time. I laugh a good deal more than I mope. Anything really horrible has a ludicrous side—it's like Mark Twain's humour—a gross exaggeration. The maddest thing of all to me is that a person so willing to be amiable as I am should be out here killing people for principle's sake.

There's no rhyme or reason—it can't be argued. Dimly one thinks he sees what is right and leaves father and mother and home, as though it were for the Kingdom of Heaven's sake. Perhaps it is. If one didn't pin his faith to that "perhaps." One can't explain.

A merry Christmas to you.
Yours very sincerely,
Coningsby Dawson.

35

December 20th, 1916.

Dear Mr. A. D.:

I've just come in from an argument with Fritz when your chocolate formed my meal. You were very kind to think of me and to send it, and you were extraordinarily understanding in the letter that you sent me. One's life out here is like a pollarded tree—all the lower branches are gone—one gazes on great nobilities, on the fascinating horror of Eternity sometimes—I said horror, but it's often fine in its spaciousness—one gazes on many inverted splendours of Titans, but it's giddy work being so high and rarefied, and all the gentle past seems gone.

That's why it is pleasant in this grimy anonymity of death and courage to get reminders, such as your letter, that one was once localised and had a familiar history. If I come back, I shall be like Rip Van Winkle, or a Robinson Crusoe—like any and all of the creatures of legend and history to whom abnormality has grown to seem normal. If you can imagine yourself living in a world in which every day is a demonstration of a Puritan's conception of what happens when the last trump sounds, then you have some idea of my queer situation.

One has come to a point when death seems very inconsiderable and only failure to do one's duty is an utter loss. Love and the future, and all the sweet and tender dreams of bygone days are like a house in which the blinds are lowered and from which the sight has gone. Landscapes have lost their beauty, everything God-made and man-made is destroyed except man's power to endure with a smile the things he once most dreaded, because he believes that only so may he be righteous in his own eyes.

How one has longed for that sure confidence in the petty failings of little living—the confidence to believe that he can stand up and suffer for principle! God has given all men who are out here that opportunity—the supremest that can be hoped for—so, in spite of exile, Christmas for most of us will be a happy day. Does one see more truly life's worth on a battlefield? I often ask myself that question. Is the contempt that is hourly shown for life the real standard of life's worth? I shrug my shoulders at my own unanswerable questions—all I know is that I move daily with men who have everything to live for who, nevertheless, are urged by an unconscious magnanimity to die. I don't think any of our dead pity themselves—but they would have done so if they had faltered in their choice. One lives only from sunrise to sunrise, but there's a more real happiness in this brief living than I ever knew before, because it is so exactingly worthwhile.

Thank you again for your kindness.

Very sincerely yours,

C. D.

The suggestion that we might all meet in London in January, 1917, was a hope rather than an expectation. We received a cable from France on Sunday, December 17th, 1916, and left New York on December 30th. We were met in London by the two sailor-sons, who were expecting appointments at any moment, and Coningsby arrived late in the evening of January 13th. He was unwell when he arrived, having had a near touch of pneumonia.

The day before he left the front he had been in action, with a temperature of 104. There were difficulties about getting his leave at the exact time appointed, but these he overcame by exchanging leave with a brother-officer. He travelled from the front all night in a windowless train, and at Calais was delayed by a draft of infantry which he had to take over to England.

The consequence of this delay was that the meeting at the railway station, of which he had so long dreamed, did not come off. We spent a long day, going from station to station, misled by imperfect information as to the arrival of troop trains. At Victoria Station we saw two thousand troops arrive on leave, men caked with trench-mud, but he was not among them. We reluctantly returned to our hotel in the late afternoon and gave up expecting him. There was all the time a telegram at the hotel from him, giving the exact place and time of his arrival, but it was not delivered until it was too late to meet him. He arrived at ten o'clock, and at the same time his two brothers, who had been summoned in the morning to Southampton, entered the hotel, having been granted special leave to return to London. A night's rest did wonders for Coningsby and the next day his spirits were as high as in the old days of joyous holiday.

During the next eight days we lived at a tense pitch of excitement. We went to theatres, dined in restaurants, met friends, and heard from his lips a hundred details of his life which could not be communicated in letters. We were all thrilled by the darkened heroic London through which we moved, the London which bore its sorrows so proudly, and went about its daily life with such silent courage.

We visited old friends to whom the war had brought irreparable bereavements, but never once heard the voice of self-pity, of murmur or complaint. To me it was an incredible England; an England purged of all weakness, stripped of flabbiness, regenerated by sacrifice.

I had dreamed of no such transformation by anything I had read in American newspapers and magazines. I think no one can imagine the completeness of this rebirth of the soul of England who has not dwelt, if only for a few days, among its people.

Coningsby's brief leave expired all too soon. We saw him off from Folkestone, and while we were saying goodbye to him, his two brothers were on their way to their distant appointments with the Royal Naval Motor Patrol in the North of Scotland. We left Liverpool for New York on January 27th, and while at sea heard of the diplomatic break between America and Germany. The news was received on board the S. S. St Paul with rejoicing. It was Sunday, and the religious service on board concluded with the Star-Spangled Banner.

December 28th, 1916.

Dearest All:

I'm writing you this letter because I expect tonight is a busy-packing one with you. The picture is in my mind of you all. How splendid it is of you to come! I never thought you would really, not even in my wildest dream of optimism. There have been so many times when I scarcely thought that I would ever see you again—now the unexpected and hoped-for happens. It's ripping!

I've put in an application for special leave in case the ordinary leave should be cut off. I think I'm almost certain to arrive by the 11th. Won't we have a time? I wonder what we'll want to do most—sit quiet or go to theatres? The nine days of freedom—the wonderful nine days—will pass with most tragic quickness. But they'll be days to remember as long as life lasts.

Shall I see you standing on the station when I puff into London—or will it be Folkestone where we meet—or shall I arrive before you?

I somehow think it will be you who will meet me at the barrier at Charing Cross, and we'll taxi through the darkened streets down the Strand, and back to our privacy. How impossible it sounds—like a vision of heart's desire in the night.

Far, far away I see the fine home-coming, like a lamp burning in a dark night. I expect we shall all go off our heads with joy and be madder than ever. Who in the old London days would have imagined such a nine days of happiness in the old places as we are to have together. God bless you, till we meet,

Con.

37

January 4th, 1917.

10.30 p.m.

My Dearest Ones:

This letter is written to welcome you to England, but I may be with you when it is opened.

It was glorious news to hear that you were coming—I was only playing a forlorn bluff when I sent those cables. You're on the sea at present and should be half way over. Our last trip over together you marvelled at the apparent indifference of the soldiers on board, and now you're coming to meet one of your own fresh from the front. A change!

O what a nine days we're going to have together—the most wonderful that were ever spent. I dream of them, tell myself tales about them, live them over many times in imagination be- fore they are realised. Sometimes I'm going to have no end of sleep, sometimes I'm going to keep awake every second, sometimes I'm going to sit quietly by a fire, and sometimes I'm going to taxi all the time. I can't fit your faces into the picture—it seems too unbelievable that we are to be together once again.

Today I've been staging our meeting—if you arrive first, and then if I arrive before you, and lastly if we both hit London on the same day. You mustn't expect me to be a sane person. You're three rippers to do this—and I hope you'll have an easy journey. The only ghost is the last day, when the leave train pulls out of Charing Cross. But we'll do that smiling, too; *C'est la guerre.*

Yours always and ever, Con.

38

January 6th, 1917.

My Dear Ones:

I have just seen a brother officer aboard the ex-London bus *en route* for Blighty. How I wished I could have stepped on board that ex-London perambulator tonight! "Pickerdilly Cirkuss, 'Ighbury, 'Ighgate, Welsh 'Arp—all the wye."

O my, what a time I'll have when I meet you! I shall feel as though if anything happens to me after my return you'll be able to understand so much more bravely. These blinkered letters, with only writing and no touch of live hands, convey so little. When we've had a good time together and sat round the fire and talked interminably you'll be able to read so much more between the lines of my future letters. Tomorrow you ought to land in England, and tomorrow night you should sleep in London. I am trying to swop my leave with another man, otherwise it won't come till the 15th.

I am looking forward every hour to those miraculous nine days which we are to have together. You can't imagine with your vividest imagination the contrast between nine days with you in London and my days where I am now. A battalion went by yesterday, marching into action, and its band was playing *I've a Sneakin' Feelin' in My Heart That I Want to Settle Down*. We all have that sneaking feeling from time to time. I tell myself wonderful stories in the early dark mornings and become the architect of the most wonderful futures.

I'm coming to join you just as soon as I know how—at the worst I'll be in London on the 16th of this month.

Ever yours.
Con.

The following letters were written after Coningsby had met his family in London.

39

January 24th, 1917.
My Dear Ones:
I have had a chance to write you sooner than I expected, as I stopped the night where I disembarked, and am catching my train today.

It's strange to be back and under orders after nine days' freedom. Directly I landed I was detailed to march a party, it was that that made me lose my train—not that I objected, for I got one more sleep between sheets. I picked up on the boat in the casual way one does, with three other officers, so on landing we made a party to dine together, and had a very decent evening. I wasn't wanting to remember too much then, so that was why I didn't write letters.

What good times we have to look back on and how much to be thankful for, that we met altogether. Now we must look forward to the summer and, perhaps, the end of the war. What a mad joy will sweep across the world on the day that peace is declared!

This visit will have made you feel that you have a share in all that's happening over here and are as real a part of it as any of us. I'm awfully proud of you for your courage.

Yours lovingly.

Con.

40

January 26th, 1917.

My Very Dear Ones:

Here I am back—my nine days' leave a dream. I got into our wagon-lines last night after midnight, having had a cold ride along frozen roads through white wintry country. I was only half-expected, so my sleeping-bag hadn't been unpacked. I had to wake my batman and tramp about a mile to the billet; by the time I got there every one was asleep, so I spread out my sleeping-sack and crept In very quietly.

For the few minutes before my eyes closed I pictured London, the taxis, the gay parties, the mystery of lights. I was roused this morning with the news that I had to go up to the gun-position at once. I stole just sufficient time to pick up a part of my accumulated mail, then got on my horse and set out. At the guns, I found that I was due to report as liaison officer, so here I am in the trenches again writing to you by candle-light. How wonderfully we have bridged the distance in spending those nine whole days together. And now it is over, and I am back in the trenches, and tomorrow you're sailing for New York.

I can't tell you what the respite has meant to me. There have been times when my whole past life has seemed a myth and the future an endless prospect of carrying on. Now I can distantly hope that the old days will return.

When I was in London half my mind was at the front; now that I'm back in the trenches half my mind is in London. I relive our gay times together; I go to cosy little dinners; I sit with you in the stalls, listening to the music; then I tumble off to sleep, and dream, and wake up to find the dream a delusion. It's a fine and manly contrast, however, between the game one plays out here and the fretful trivialities of civilian life.

41

January 27th.

I got as far as this and then "something" happened. Twenty-four hours have gone by and once more it's nearly midnight and I write to you by candle-light. Since last night I've been with these infantry boy-officers who are doing such great work in such a careless spirit of jolliness. Any softness which had crept into me during my nine days of happiness has gone. I'm glad to be out here and wouldn't wish to be anywhere else till the war is ended.

It's a week today since we were at *Charlie's Aunt*—such a cheerful little party! I expect the boys are doing their share of remembering too somewhere on the sea at present. I know you are, as you round the coast of Ireland and set out for the Atlantic.

I've not been out of my clothes for three days and I've another day to go yet. I brought my haversack into the trenches with me; on opening it I found that some kind hands had slipped into it some clean socks and a bottle of Horlick's Malted Milk tablets.

The signallers in a nearby dugout are singing *Keep the Home-Fires Burning Till the Boys Come Home*. That's what we're all doing, isn't it—you at your end and we at ours? The brief few days of possessing myself are over and once more stem duty lies ahead.

But I thank God for the chance I've had to see again those whom I love, and to be able to tell them with my own lips some of the bigness of our life at the front. No personal aims count beside the great privilege which is ours to carry on until the war is over.

All my thoughts are with you—so many memories of kindness. I keep on picturing things I ought to have done—things I ought to have told you.

Always I can see. Oh, so vividly, the two sailor brothers waving goodbye as the train moved off through the London dusk, and then that other and forlorner group of three, standing outside the dock gates with the sentry like the angel in Eden, turning them back from happiness. With an extraordinary aloofness I watched myself moving like a puppet away from you whom I love most dearly in all the world—going away as if going were a thing so usual.

I'm asking myself again if there isn't some new fineness of spirit which will develop from this war and survive it. In London, at a distance from all this tragedy of courage, I felt that I had slipped back to a lower plane; a kind of flabbiness was creeping into my blood—the old selfish fear of life and love of comfort. It's odd that out here, where the fear of death should supplant the fear of life, one somehow rises into a contempt for everything which is not bravest. There's no doubt that the call for sacrifice, and perhaps the supreme sacrifice, can transform men into a nobility of which they themselves are unconscious. That's the most splendid thing of all, that they themselves are unaware of their fineness.

I'm now waiting to be relieved and am hurrying to finish this so that I may mail it as soon as I get back to the battery. There's a whole sack of letters and parcels waiting for me there, and I'm as eager to get to them as a kiddy to inspect his Christmas stocking. I always undo the string and wrappings with a kind of reverence, trying to picture the dear kneeling figures who did them up. In London I didn't dare to let myself go with you—I couldn't say all that was in my heart—it wouldn't have been wise. Don't ever doubt that the tenderness was there. Even though one is only a civilian in khaki, some of the soldier's sternness becomes second nature.

All the country is covered with snow—it's brilliant clear weather, more like America than Europe. I'm feeling strong as a horse, ever so much better than I felt when on leave. Life is really tremendously worth living, in spite of the war.

January 28th.

I'm back at the battery, sitting by a cosy fire. I might be up at Kootenay by the look of my surroundings. I'm in a shack with a really truly floor, and a window looking out on moonlit whiteness. If it wasn't for the tapping of the distant machine guns—tapping that always sounds to me like the nailing up of coffins—I might be here for pleasure. In imagination I can see your great ship, with all its portholes aglare, ploughing across the darkness to America.

The dear sailor brothers I can't quite visualise; I can only see them looking so upright and pale when we said goodbye. It's getting late and the fire's dying. I'm half asleep; I've not been out of my clothes for three nights. I shall tell myself a story of the end of the war and our next meeting—it'll last from the time that I creep into my sack until I close my eyes. It's a glorious life.

Yours very lovingly.
Con

43

January 31st, 1917.

Dear Mr. and Mrs. M.:

It was extremely good of you to remember me. I got back from leave in London on the 26th and found the cigarettes waiting for me. One hasn't got an awful lot of pleasures left, but smoking is one of them. I feel particularly doggy when I open my case and find my initials on them.

I expect you'll have heard all the news of my leave long before this reaches you. We had a splendid time and the greatest of luck. My sailor brothers were with me all but two days, and my people were in England only a few days before I arrived.

This is a queer adventure for a peaceable person like myself—it blots out all the past and reduces the future to a speck. One hardly hopes that things will ever be different, but looks forward to interminable years of carrying on. My leave rather corrected that frame of mind; it came as a surprise to be forced to realise that not all the world was living under orders on womanless, childless battlefields. But we don't need any pity—we manage our good times, and are sorry for the men who aren't here, for it's a wonderful thing to have been chosen to sacrifice and perhaps to die that the world of the future may be happier and kinder.

This letter is rather disjointed; I'm in charge of the battery for the time, and messages keep on coming in, and one has to rush out to give the order to fire.

It's an American night—snow-white and piercing, with a frigid moon sailing quietly. I think the quiet beauty of the sky is about the only thing in Nature that we do not scar and destroy with our fighting.

Goodbye, and thank you ever so much.

Yours very sincerely,

Coningsby Dawson.

44

February 1st, 1917.

11 p.m.

Dear Father:

Your picture of the black days when no letter comes from me sets me off scribbling to you at this late hour. All today I've been having a cold but amusing time at the O. P. (Forward Observation Post). It seems brutal to say it, but taking pot shots at the enemy when they present themselves is rather fun. When you watch them scattering like ants before the shell whose direction you have ordered, you somehow forget to think of them as individuals, any more than the bear-hunter thinks of the cubs that will be left motherless.

You watch your victims through your glasses as God might watch his mad universe. Your skill in directing fire makes you what in peace times would be called a murderer. Curious! You're glad, and yet at close quarters only in hot blood would you hurt a man.

I'd been back for a little over an hour when I had to go forward again to guide in some guns. The country was dazzlingly white in the moonlight. As far as eye could see every yard was an old battlefield; beneath the soft white fleece of snow lay countless unburied bodies. Like frantic fingers tearing at the sky, all along the horizon, Hun lights were shooting up and drifting across our front. *Tap-tap-tappity* went the machine-guns; whoo-oo went the heavies, and they always stamp like angry bulls.

I had to come back by myself across the heroic corruption which the snow had covered. All the way I asked myself why was I not frightened. What has happened to me? Ghosts should walk here if anywhere. Moreover, I know that I shall be frightened again when the war is ended. Do you remember how you once offered me money to walk through the Forest of Dean after dark, and I wouldn't? I wouldn't if you offered it to me now. You remember Meredith's lines in *The Woods of Westermain*:

All the eyeballs under hoods
Shroud you in their glare;
Enter these enchanted woods
You who dare.

Maybe what recreates one for the moment is the British officer's uniform, and even more the fact that you are not asked, but expected, to do your duty. So I came back quite unruffled across battered trenches and silent mounds to write this letter to you.

My dear father, I'm over thirty, and yet just as much a little boy as ever. I still feel overwhelmingly dependent on your good opinion and love. I'm glad that they are black days when you have no letters from me. I love to think of the rush to the door when the postman rings and the excited shouting up the stairs, "Quick, one from Con."

February 2nd.

You see by the writing how tired I was when I reached this point. It's nearly twenty-four hours later and again night. The gramophone is playing an air from *La Tosca* to which the guns

79

beat out a bass accompaniment. I close my eyes and picture the many times I have heard the (probably) German orchestras of Broadway Joy Palaces play that same music.

How incongruous that I should be listening to it here and under these circumstances! It must have been listened to so often by gay crowds in the beauty places of the world. A romantic picture grows up in my mind of a blue night, the laughter of youth in evening dress, lamps twinkling through trees, far off the velvety shadow of water and mountains, and as a voice to it all, that air from *La Tosco*.

I can believe that the silent people nearby raise themselves up in their snow-beds to listen, each one recalling some ecstatic moment before the dream of life was shattered.

There's a picture in the Pantheon at Paris, I remember; I believe it's called *To Glory*, One sees all the armies of the ages charging out of the middle distance with Death riding at their head. The only glory that I have discovered in this war is in men's hearts—it's not external. Were one to paint the spirit of this war he would depict a mud landscape, blasted trees, an iron sky; wading through the slush and shell-holes would come a file of bowed figures, more like outcasts from the embankment than soldiers. They're loaded down like pack animals, their shoulders are rounded, they're wearied to death, but they go on and go on.

There's no "To Glory" about what we're doing out here; there's no flash of swords or splendour of uniforms. There are only very tired men determined to carry on. The war will be won by tired men who could never again pass an insurance test, a mob of broken counter-jumpers, ragged ex-plumbers and quite unheroic persons. We're civilians in khaki, but because of the ideals for which we fight we've managed to acquire soldiers' hearts.

My flow of thought was interrupted by a burst of song in which I was compelled to join. We're all writing letters around one candle; suddenly the O. C. looked up and began, *God Be With You Till We Meet Again*. We sang it in parts. It was in Southport, when I was about nine years old, that I first heard that sung. You had gone for your first trip to America, leaving a very lonely family behind you. We children were scared to death that you'd be drowned.

One evening, coming back from a walk on the sand-hills, we heard voices singing in a garden, *God Be With You Till We Meet Again*. The words and the soft dusk, and the vague figures in the English summer garden, seemed to typify the terror of all partings. We've said goodbye so often since, and God has been with us. I don't think any parting was more hard than our last at the prosaic dock-gates with the cold wind of duty blowing, and the sentry barring your entrance, and your path leading back to America while mine led on to France.

But you three were regular soldiers—just as much soldiers as we chaps who were embarking. One talks of our armies in the field, but there are the other armies, millions strong, of mothers and fathers and sisters, who keep their eyes dry, treasure muddy letters beneath their pillows, offer up prayers and wait, wait, wait so eternally for God to open another door.

Tomorrow I again go forward, which means rising early and taking a long plod through the snows; that's one reason for not writing any more, and another is that our one poor candle is literally on its last legs.

Your poem, written years ago when the poor were marching in London, is often in my mind:

Yesterday and today
Have been heavy with labour and sorrow;
I should faint if I did not see
The day that is after tomorrow.

And there's that last verse which prophesied utterly the spirit in which we men at the front are fighting today:

And for me, with spirit elate
The mire and the fog I press thorough.
For Heaven shines under the cloud
Of the day that is after tomorrow.

We civilians who have been taught so long to love our enemies and do good to them who hate us—much too long ever to make professional soldiers—are watching with our hearts in our eyes for that day which comes after tomorrow. Meanwhile we plod on determinedly, hoping for the hidden glory.

Yours very lovingly.
Con.

45

February 3rd, 1917.

Dear Misses W.:

You were very kind to remember me at Christmas. *Seventeen* was read with all kinds of gusto by all my brother officers. It's still being borrowed.

I've been back from leave a few days now and am settling back to business again. It was a trifle hard after over-eating and undersleeping myself for nine days, and riding everywhere with my feet up in taxis. I was the wildest little boy. Here it's snowy and bitter. We wear scarves round our ears to keep the frost away and dream of fires a mile high. All I ask, when the war is ended, is to be allowed to sit asleep in a big armchair and to be left there absolutely quiet. Sleep, which we crave so much at times, is only death done up in sample bottles. Perhaps some of these very weary men who strew our battlefields are glad to lie at last at endless leisure. Goodbye, and thank you.

Yours very sincerely,
Con.

46

February 4th, 1917.

My Dearest Mother:

Somewhere in the distance I can hear a piano going and men's voices singing *A Perfect Day*. It's queer how music creates a world for you in which you are not, and makes you dreamy. I've been sitting by a fire and thinking of all the happy times when the total of desire seemed almost within one's grasp. It never is—one always, always misses it and has to rub the dust from the eyes, recover one's breath and set out on the search afresh. I suppose when you grow very old you learn the lesson of sitting quiet, and the heart stops beating and the total of desire comes to you.

And yet I can remember so many happy days, when I was a child in the summer and later at Kootenay. One almost thought he had caught the secret of carrying heaven in his heart.

By the time this reaches you I'll be in the line again, but for the present I'm undergoing a special course of training. You can't hear the most distant sound of guns, and if it wasn't for the pressure of study, similar to that at Kingston, one would be very rested.

Sunday of all days is the one when I remember you most. You're just sitting down to midday dinner,—I've made the calculation for difference of time. You're probably saying how less than a month ago we were in London. That doesn't sound true even when I write it. I wonder how your old familiar surroundings strike you. It's terrible to come down from the mountain heights of a great elation like our ten days in London. I often think of that with regard to myself when the war is ended. There'll be a sense of dissatisfaction when the old lost comforts are regained.

There'll be a sense of lowered manhood. The stupendous terrors of Armageddon demand less courage than the uneventful terror of the daily commonplace. There's something splendid and exhilarating in going forward among bursting shells—we, who have done all that, know that when the guns have ceased to roar our blood will grow more sluggish and we'll never be such men again. Instead of getting up in the morning and hearing your O. C. say, "You'll run a line into trench so-and-so today and shoot up such-and-such Hun wire," you'll hear necessity saying, "You'll work from breakfast to dinner and earn your daily bread. And you'll do it tomorrow and tomorrow and tomorrow world without end. Amen."

They never put that forever and forever part into their commands out here, because the Amen for any one of us may be only a few hours away. But the big immediate thing is so much easier to do than the prosaic carrying on without anxiety—which is your game. I begin to understand what you have had to suffer now that R. and E. are really at war too. I get awfully anxious about them. I never knew before that either of them owned so much of my heart.

I get furious when I remember that they might get hurt. I've heard of a Canadian who joined when he learnt that his best friend had been murdered by Hun bayonets. He came to get his own back and was the most reckless man in his battalion. I can understand his temper now. We're all of us in danger of slipping back into the worship of Thor.

I'll write as often as I can while here, but I don't get much time—so you'll understand. It's the long nights when one sits up to take the firing in action that give one the chance to be a decent correspondent.

My birthday comes round soon, doesn't it? Good heavens, how ancient I'm getting and without any "grow old along with me" consolation. Well, to grow old is all in the job of living.

Good-bye, and God bless you all

Yours ever.

Con.

47

February 4th, 1917.

Dear Mr. B.:

I have been intending to write to you for a very long time, but as most of one's writing is done when one ought to be asleep, and sleep next to eating is one of our few remaining pleasures, my intended letter has remained in my head up to now. On returning from a nine days' leave to London the other day, however, I found two letters from you awaiting me and was reproached into effort.

War's a queer game—not at all what one's civilian mind imagined; it's far more horrible and less exciting. The horrors which the civilian mind dreads most are mutilation and death. Out here we rarely think about them; the thing which wears on one most and calls out his gravest courage is the endless sequence of physical discomfort. Not to be able to wash, not to be able to sleep, to have to be wet and cold for long periods at a stretch, to find mud on your person, in your food, to have to stand in mud, see mud, sleep in mud and to continue to smile—that's what tests courage.

Our chaps are splendid. They're not the hair-brained idiots that some war-correspondents depict from day to day. They're perfectly sane people who know to a fraction what they're up against, but who carry on with a grim good-nature and a determination to win with a smile. I never before appreciated as I do today the latent capacity for big-hearted endurance that is in the heart of every man.

Here are apparently quite ordinary chaps—chaps who washed, liked theatres, loved kiddies and sweethearts, had a zest for life—they're bankrupt of all pleasures except the supreme pleasure of knowing that they're doing the ordinary and finest thing of which they are capable. There are millions to whom the mere consciousness of doing their duty has brought an heretofore unexperienced peace of mind. For myself I was never happier than I am at present; there's a novel zip added to life by the daily risks and the knowledge that at last you're doing something into which no trace of selfishness enters.

One can only die once; the chief concern that matters is how and not when you die. I don't pity the weary men who have attained eternal leisure in the corruption of our shell-furrowed battles; they "went west" in their supreme moment. The men I pity are those who could not hear the call of duty and whose consciences will grow more flabby every day. With the brutal roar of the first Prussian gun the cry came to the civilised world, "*Follow thou me*," just as truly as it did in Palestine.

Men went to their Calvary singing *Tipperary*, rubbish, rhymed doggerel, but their spirit was equal to that of any Christian martyr in a Roman amphitheatre. "*Greater love hath no man than this, that he lay down his life for his friend."* Our chaps are doing that consciously, willingly, almost without bitterness towards their enemies; for the rest it doesn't matter whether they sing hymns or ragtime.

They've followed their ideal—freedom—and died for it. A former age expressed itself in Gregorian chants; ours, no less sincerely, disguises its feelings in ragtime.

Since September I have been less than a month out of action. The game doesn't pall as time goes on—it fascinates. We've got to win so that men may never again be tortured by the ingenious inquisition of modem warfare. The winning of the war becomes a personal affair to the chaps who are fighting.

The world which sits behind the lines, buys extra specials of the daily papers and eats three square meals a day, will never know what this other world has endured for its safety, for no man of this other world will have the vocabulary in which to tell. But don't for a moment mistake me—we're grimly happy.

What a serial I'll write for you if I emerge from this turmoil! Thank God, my outlook is all altered. I don't want to live any longer—only to live well.

Goodbye and good luck.

Yours,

Coningsby Dawson.

48

February 5th, 1917.

My Dearest Mother:

Aren't the papers good reading now-a-days with nothing to record but success? It gives us hope that at last, anyway before the year is out, the war must end. As you know, I am at the artillery school back of the lines for a month, taking an extra course. I have been meeting a great many young officers from all over the world and have listened to them discussing their program for when peace is declared. Very few of them have any plans or prospects.

Most of them had just started on some course of professional training to which they won't have the energy to go back after a two years' interruption. The question one asks is how will all these men be reabsorbed into civilian life. I'm afraid the result will be a vast host of men with promising pasts and highly uncertain futures. We shall be a holiday world without an income. I'm afraid the hero-worship attitude will soon change to impatience when the soldiers beat their swords into ploughshares and then confess that they have never been taught to plough. That's where I shall score—by beating my sword into a pen.

But what to write about! Everything will seem so little and inconsequential after seeing armies marching to mud and death, and people will soon get tired of hearing about that. It seems as though war does to the individual what it does to the landscapes it attacks—obliterates everything personal and characteristic. A valley, when a battle has done with it, is nothing but earth—exactly what it was when God said, "*Let there be Light;*" a man just something with a mind purged of the past and ready to observe afresh. I question whether a return to old environments will ever restore to us the whole of our old tastes and affections.

War is, I think, utterly destructive. It doesn't even create courage—it only finds it in the soul of a man. And yet there is one quality which will survive the war and help us to face the temptations of peace—that same courage which most of us have un- consciously discovered out here.

Well, my dear, I have little news—at least, none that I can tell. I'm just about recovered from an attack of "flu." I want to get thoroughly rid of it before I go back to my battery. I hope you all keep well. God bless you all.

Yours ever.
Con.

49

February 6th, 1917.
My Very Dear M.:
I read in today's paper that U. S. A. threatens to come over and help us. I wish she would. The very thought of the possibil-

ity fills me with joy. I've been light-headed all day. It would be so ripping to live among people, when the war is ended, of whom you need not be ashamed. Somewhere deep down in my heart I've felt a sadness ever since I've been out here, at America's lack of gallantry—it's so easy to find excuses for not climbing to Calvary; sacrifice was always too noble to be sensible. I would like to see the country of our adoption become splendidly irrational even at this eleventh hour in the game; it would redeem her in the world's eyes. She doesn't know what she's losing.

From these carcase-strewn fields of khaki there's a cleansing wind blowing for the nations that have died. Though there was only one Englishman left to carry on the race when this war is victoriously ended, I would give more for the future of England than for the future of America with her ninety millions whose sluggish blood was not stirred by the call of duty. It's bigness of soul that makes nations great and not population. Money, comfort, limousines and ragtime are not the requisites of men when heroes are dying.

I hate the thought of Fifth Avenue, with its pretty faces, its fashions, its smiling frivolity. America as a great nation will die, as all coward civilisations have died, unless she accepts the stigmata of sacrifice, which a divine opportunity again offers her.

If it were but possible to show those ninety millions one battlefield with its sprawling dead, its pity, its marvellous forgetfulness of self, I think then—no, they wouldn't be afraid. Fear isn't the emotion one feels—they would experience the shame of living when so many have shed their youth freely. This war is a prolonged moment of exultation for most of us—we are redeeming ourselves in our own eyes.

To lay down one's life for one's friend once seemed impossible. All that is altered. We lay down our lives that the future generations may be good and kind, and so we can contemplate oblivion with quiet eyes. Nothing that is noblest that the Greeks taught is unpractised by the simplest men out here today. They may die childless, but their example will father the imagination of all the coming ages. These men, in the noble indignation of a great ideal, face a worse hell than the most ingenious of fanatics ever planned or plotted.

Men die scorched like moths in a furnace, blown to atoms, gassed, tortured. And again other men step forward to take their places well knowing what will be their fate. Bodies may die, but the spirit of England grows greater as each new soul speeds upon its way. The battened souls of America will die and be buried. I believe the decision of the next few days will prove to be the crisis in America's nationhood. If she refuses the pain which will save her, the cancer of self-despising will rob her of her life.

This feeling is strong with us. It's past midnight but I could write of nothing else tonight.

God bless you.

Yours ever.

Con.

Living Bayonets

Contents

"OUR SPIRITS ARE LIVING BAYONETS. THE
IDEALS WHICH WE CARRY IN OUR HEARTS
ARE MORE DEADLY TO THE ENEMY
THAN ANY MAN-MADE WEAPONS."

Foreword

These selections from collected letters of Coningsby Dawson to his family, have been edited by his sister, Muriel Dawson, and are published in response to hundreds of requests. Readers of his first volume of correspondence from the front, issued under the title of *Carry On*, have written from all over the country asking that a further series be given them. The generous appreciation and personal interest expressed by these readers, have induced Lieutenant Coningsby Dawson's family to publish these letters. They take up his story at the point where *Carry On* laid it down, at the time when America entered the war.

The Letters

1

France
April 14, 1917

The other night at twelve your letters came to me just as I was climbing into my bunk, so recently tenanted by a Hun. I immediately lit another candle, stuck it on the wall in a manner peculiar to myself, and started on a feast of genuine home gossip.

What a difference it must make to you to know that the United States are at last confessedly our Ally. Their financial and industrial support will be invaluable to us and will make a difference at once. And the moral advantage of having them on our side is the greatest wound to the spirit of Germany that she has received since the war started. It will be real fun to be able to come back to New York in khaki, won't it?—instead of slinking in as a civilian. Besides, if I get wounded, I'll be able to come home to visit you on leave now.

This big decision has made me almost gay ever since it happened. I have such a new affection for everything across the Atlantic—almost as if New York and the Hudson were just across the lawn from England, the nearest of near neighbours. I wish with all my heart that I could drop in on you for a day and just sit down on the sunny veranda and talk and talk. There's so much I want to hear and so much I want to understand in the changed attitude of America. I'm sure everyone must be much more happy now that the cloud of reproach has lifted and the brightness of heroism is in the air. It shines in my imagination like the clear blueness above the white towers of New York. There's one thing certain; now that the president has made up his mind, the country will go as bald headedly for war as it has for everything else it ever set out to attain. The real momentousness of this happening hasn't been appreciated by the fighting men out here yet. With a sublime arrogance they feel themselves quite capable of licking Germany without the assistance of anyone.

I'm very much anticipating the arrival of the first copy of *Carry On*—not that I shall show it to anyone.

2

France
April 17, 1917

Last night I was out on a working party—a moonlight night with sleet falling, and did not get back till past two. The first thing my flashlight fell on as I entered my dugout was a pile of letters from home. At past 3 a.m. I was still reading them, when H. and B. woke up and asked if there was anything for them. There was. So there we were all lying in our bunks and reading our love-letters till nearly 4 a.m.

Yesterday I had a very exciting time. I was doing some reconnoitring along the front when a bullet whizzed by and almost scorched the ear of my sergeant. We hopped into a trench about two feet full of water. But whenever we showed ourselves the sniping started up again. At last we got tired of wading, so climbed out and made a dash across the open. None of us were caught, but by pure bad luck another sergeant of mine who was waiting quite 300 yards away, got it in the back. He was a big, heavy chap and we had quite a slippery time carrying him out on a stretcher to the dressing-station.

That's the second N.C.O. who's been hit with me in the last ten days. The other chap got it in his side. Either of these wounds would have been nice to get for anyone who wanted a rest. But I don't want to get out yet; all the really sporting part of this war will be this summer. We are praying that we may come into action at the gallop, "Halt, action front!" bang off our rounds and follow up again.

For some reason, today my memory has been full of pictures of that wonderful leave we had together in London. Things have come back that I'd forgotten—visits to theatres, to restaurants, rides in taxis, so many things—all the time there's that extraordinary atmosphere of intense love. I suppose I must have spent the night dreaming of you. Living in the daylight hours in this deep dugout makes spring seem like winter; I expect that helps me to remember.

How I wish I could have those ten days again. Perhaps our next will be in New York, when I come back in khaki for an odd week. The thought of such a happening in the future and the recollection of the meeting that is past are like coming to a fire out of a dark cold night. This war is so monstrously impersonal; the attachments one forms with those among whom he lives are so few, that the passionately personal affections of the old days shine out like beacon fires. It will be wonderful when the war ends and one can sit still in a great hush.

Yesterday I had a day off for a bath behind the lines—I hadn't tubbed for well over a month and hadn't been back of the guns; also I had slept in my clothes—so you may judge that warm water and soap were a necessity. Afterwards I had great fun shopping for the mess, but I didn't manage to buy much as the country is all eaten up. All that is beautiful in the way of landscape lies ahead, so we're very anxious to capture it from the Hun. One looks out over his back country, so green and beautiful and untouched, and feels like an Old Testament spy having a peep at the Promised Land.

Without doubt it will be ours in the ordained time. When I went out this morning it was to see a blue, blue sky, a battery pulling into action and behind it a desolated town. But the feature that caught my attention was the spring sky. I stared and stared at it and thought of when the war is ended. Today I had to go to another town which is in process of being battered. On my way back I passed through a wood—most of the trees were levelled to the ground. In the wood I found a hawk wounded by shrapnel, and pressing close behind a fallen trunk. And I found my first spring flower—a daffodil—which I am enclosing to you. I've sent you many flowers, but none which carries with it more love than this little withered daffodil—my first token of spring—gathered from a fought-over woodland of France.

Since writing thus far it has been raining cats and dogs, and I've been catching the mud, which leaks through my roof, in a soup-plate. Little things like mud and rain don't damp our ardour, however; we press on and on to certain victory. One of our officers came back from leave today—he'd spent his freedom in Devon, and was full of the beauty of the springtime there. Happy Devon! War has changed the seasons in France. Winter started in October; it's the middle of April and winter has not yet ended. Oh, to wake up again with the splendid assurance of a summer day with nothing but beauty—such a peaceful day as we have so often spent at Kootenay.

That wounded hawk, crouching among the daffodils, is a symbol—we're like that: beasts of prey for our country's sake, maimed in mind and spirit, and waiting till our wings grow strong again. And yet—Who would be anywhere else but here so long as the war lasts? Oh, the fine clean courage of the men in the face of danger and their brave endurance in the presence of privation! It passes understanding. I saw a chap with a mortal wound the other day thinking nothing of himself—only of his pal, who was but slightly wounded. The most unendurable' people act like heroes in the face of death. There's a fundamental nobility in all men which comes to the surface when life is most despairing.

3

France
April 19, 1917

I sit in a hole in a recent battlefield. Over my head is some tattered canvas, upheld by Fritzie shovels. In a battered bucket wood splutters, and the rain it raineth every day. To make my appearance more gipsy-like I may add that my hands are cracked with the mud. When the war is ended I shall lie in bed for a month.

We've come through some very lively times of late, and I shall have plenty of local colour to impart to you when the war is ended. My mind is packed with vivid pictures which I cannot tell. This huge silence which rests between individuals is the most terrific thing about the war. You get the terror made concrete for you when you creep to your observation post and spy upon the Hun country. In the foreground is a long stretch of barbed wire, shell-holes and mud. Behind that a ruined town; then gradually, greenness growing more vivid as it recedes to the horizon.

Nothing stirs. You may look through your telescope all day, but nothing stirs. Yet you know that in every hole the hidden death lurks; should you for a moment forget and raise your head unwarily, you are reminded of your folly by the crack of a rifle. I've always made the mistake of believing the best of everyone—and, as a soldier, I've never been able to credit the fact that any-one of a big nation would count himself happy to get my scalp. The actual passes belief.

I recall so vividly that story of the final war, written by a German, *The Human Slaughter-house*. The chap never realizes the awfulness of his job until for the first time he comes face to face with the young boy he's called upon to kill.

We kill by hundreds from a distance, but the destroyed and the destroyers rarely have a hint of each other's identity. I came to a dugout the other day in a battered trench. Even the water in the shell-holes was dyed by explosives to the colour of blood. Outside lay a German, face downwards in the mud—an old man with grizzled hair.

I shoved my revolver round the mouth of the dugout and called to anyone who was there to come out. A Cockney voice answered; then followed a scrambling; two huge feet came up through the dark; they belonged to a dead German; two of his comrades grinned cheerfully at me from behind the corpse and propelled it none too reverently into the mud.

Behind the party I discovered my Cockney-adventurer—a machine-gunner who, having lost his company, made amends by capturing three Fritzies and killing two others with the aid of a pal with a shattered leg. I told him to bring his pal up.

Under his directions the Fritzies trotted back into the hole and brought out the wounded fellow. They were extraordinarily meek-looking and quite surprisingly gentle; when I'd told them where the dressing-station was, they made a bandy-chair of their hands, placed our fellow's arms about their necks and staggered away through the barrage—or curtain of fire, as the papers like to call it—back to safety with their wounded enemy. And yet within the hour all these people had been chucking bombs at one another.

A few days ago I was detailed for a novel experience—to follow up the infantry attack across No Man's Land to the Hun front line and as far as his support trenches. I called for volunteers to accompany me and had a splendid lot of chaps. My party got away with the adventure without a scratch—which was extraordinarily lucky. Moreover we accomplished the particular job that we were called upon to do.

Tonight I'm out from dusk to daylight poking through the darkness in a country where one dare not use a flashlight. Between two ruined towns I have to pass a battered calvary. The Christ upon His Cross is still untouched, though the shrine and surrounding trees are smashed to atoms. I think He means more to me like that—stripped of His gorgeousness—than ever. He seems so like ourselves in His lonely and unhallowed suffering. The road which leads to and from Him is symbolic—shell-torn, scattered with dead horses and men, while ahead the snarl of shrapnel darts across the sky and spends itself in little fleecy puffs.

All this desolation will be recreated one day, the country will grow green and, in another country, greener than any upon earth, those dead men will walk and laugh—and in that other country the Christ will no longer hang alone and aloofly.

I like to think of that—of the beauty in the future, if not in this, then in some other world. One grows tired, just like that image on the Cross. How little the body counts! War teaches us that.

4

France
April 22, 1917

I had a letter from each one of you the day before last, and they reached me within three weeks of being written—it made you all seem very near.

I am writing this to you from a mercifully deep dug-out, which was the home of Huns considerably less than a fortnight ago. I'm sure it was very obliging of them to think ahead and provide us with such safe hiding-places from their villainous shells. They have knocked the house down overhead. In the yard is a broken birdcage—the owner must have set the captive free before he made good his own escape.

Hanging at the head of my bunk is an iron crucifix and on the wall is a beautiful woman's portrait. One hardly thinks of his enemy as being human these days—he seems only an impersonal devastating force; but it was a man with affections who lately tenanted my dugout.

In a recent attack I saw a curious happening. I was up with the infantry as liaison officer when one of our planes was shot down. The pilot made an effort to land behind our trenches, but his machine was unmanageable and he came down in Boche territory—or what had been Boche territory a quarter of an hour before.

Through my glasses I saw the pilot and observer get out and start to creep cautiously back. We ourselves didn't know for certain where the Huns were—all we knew was that they were supposed to be withdrawing. When the airmen arrived at our battalion headquarters they were still scarcely convinced that our chaps were not Huns in khaki. When we gave them a meal of bully-beef they knew that we were British. So very much I could tell you which is thrilling and heroic if only I were allowed.

Do you know, sometimes I marvel at my contented loneliness? It isn't like me. I ought to be homesick and—but I'm not. I'm too much consumed with the frenzy of an ideal to care for anything but to see the principle for which we fight established. What one man can do isn't much—only a Jesus can save the world single-handed; the real satisfaction is in one's own soul, that softness and success had not made him deaf to the voice of duty when she called to him.

For me this undertaking is as holy as a crusade; if it were not I could not endure the sights. As it is I keep quiet in my soul, feeling humbly glad that I am allowed to fulfil the dreams of my boyhood. I always wanted to do something to save the world, you remember.

First I was going to be a missionary; then a reformer; then a preacher; then a poet. Instead of any of these I "struck luck" as a novelist—and I can see now how success was corroding to one's ideals. Success in America is so inevitably measured in terms of praise and money.

I wanted to save the world; never in my wildest dreams did it occur to me that I should get my chance as a soldier. I remember when I was studying history at Oxford how I used to shudder at the descriptions of battles, especially medieval battles waged by mailed Titans.

I don't know what change has taken place in me; this is a more damnable war in its possibilities for suffering than any of a by-gone age; in comparison, those old wars seem chivalrous and humane. And yet because of the spiritual goal for which we fight I no longer shudder. Yes, that is the reason for the change. A man doesn't often get the chance in these commercial times to risk all that he holds most dear for humanity's sake.

I think of the morning family prayers of childhood in the old panelled room in Highbury and the petitions you used to make for us everything has shaped towards this great moment in our lives; the past was a straight road leading to this crisis. I don't forget the share you three contribute—the share of your brave loneliness and waiting. Your share is the greatest. God bless you.

Our major was twice wounded in the recent offensives and has now left us for a higher position. I was terribly sorry to lose him.

5

France
April 30, 1917

The mud has gone. Spring is here and the sun shines all the time. Oh, a most enjoyable war, I do assure you. When I wakened this morning I wandered up the thirty stairs from my dugout into the former garden, which is now a scene of the utmost desolation. A row was going on as though the Celestial housemaid had lost her temper and given notice, and was tumbling all the plates from the pantry through the clouds.

Above the clatter I heard a sound which was almost alarming: the clear brave note of a thrush, piping, piping, piping. He didn't seem to care a rap how often the guns blew their noses or how often the Hun shrapnel clashed like cymbals overhead; he had his song to sing in the sunshine,, and was determined to sing it, no matter that the song might go unheard.

So there I stood and listened to him among the ruins, as one might listen to a faithful priest in a fallen church. I recreated in imagination the people who had lived here for generations, their tragedies, kindnesses, love-affairs. It must have been a beautiful place once, for everywhere there are stumps of fruit-trees, hedges of box trodden almost underground, circular patches which were flowerbeds.

I can picture the exiles' joy when they hear that their village has been recaptured. Presently they'll come back, these old women and men—for their sons are fighting—and they'll look in vain for even the landmarks of the little house which once sheltered their affections. The thrush in the tree is all that the Huns have left of past history. We British lose our men in the fight, but the sacrifice of the French is immeasurable, for when their sons are dead they have no quiet place of recollections.

They can't say, "Do you remember how he walked here two

years back?" or "These hollyhocks he planted," or "How he waved us goodbye as we watched him from the gate!" The same cyclone of passion which has taken their sons' lives, has robbed them of everything tangible which would remind them of him.

As regards the U.S.A. joining with us, I have spoken with several Huns. They one and all seem very dejected about it and seem to consider the loss of America's friendship one of the greatest blows of the war.

6

France
May 10, 1917

I'm just back at the guns from a two days' rest at the wagon-lines. It's the first time I've been back since March. I rose early on a blazing morning and started down to the point where I was to meet my horses. I say "rose early," but as a matter of fact I had only had four hours' sleep in forty-eight and hadn't had my clothes off for nearly three weeks. As I drew away the low thunder that we make grew less and less, the indescribable smell of bursting explosives fainter; soon I realized that a lark was singing overhead; then another then another. Brave little birds to come so near to danger to sing for us.

At the edge of a wood I found my chestnut mare, Kitty, and my groom the chap who used to work at the Silver King mine, which overlooks our ranch at Kootenay. That we should share that memory always forms a bond of kindness between us. We didn't stop long at the wagon-line, but soon started out to get further back for lunch. I had it in the shack of an officer who was with me at Petewawa. Then off I went at a gallop for green trees and clean country. I hadn't gone far before I came to a God's Acre full of crowded little white crosses and newly turned earth.

Our captain was with me and he learnt that an old friend from one of our batteries was on the way down with a Union Jack spread over him. We went into the brown field where the men who have "gone west" lie so closely and snugly side by

106

side, and came to a place where six shallow holes were dug like clay coffins. Presently, winding through the forest of crosses, the hard blue sky overhead, we saw the little band advancing, the stretcher carried high on the shoulders of four officers.

The burden was set down and the flag lifted, showing the mummy-like form sewn up in the blanket in which the living man had slept.

The chaplain began tremulously, "*I am the Resurrection and the life; he who believeth in me,*" etc., and while he recited I watched the faces of the gunners drawn up at attention in the strong sunlight. To them, whatever else the ceremony meant, it at least meant this—a day away from the guns. Suddenly I discovered that the *Lord's Prayer* was being said. Then heads were again covered and the word of command was given. "Right turn. Quick March."

The stretcher was gathered up and the little crowd dispersed. I suppose there is a woman somewhere who would have given ten years of life to have stood in my shoes beside that narrow grave.

For myself I thought, "Well, the chap's got what we long for most out here—rest. He won't have to stand in the mud any more, when his feet are like stones and eyes like lead, watching and watching the rockets go up along the front. And he won't have to guide his guns in at night or wonder what life will do to him when the war is ended. He longed for sleep and now he sleeps endlessly."

It didn't impress me as at all sad. He'd played his part like a man and was at last rewarded. But we—we were alive, and we hadn't had a bath for a month—so we jumped on our horses and trotted off to the nearest shower. It was five in the afternoon when we again took to the highway. We wanted to sponge out our minds by looking at something beautiful, just as we had sponged down our bodies.

We, I should explain, were myself and the captain of my battery. Soon we found ourselves among fields from which all the wrinkles of trenches and pit-marks of shell-holes had been smoothed out.

There was a river winding between tall trees unblasted by the curtain of fire. Peasants were at work on their little patches—women and either very old men or boys. We came to a town as quiet and unspoiled as those we used to visit in those pre-war days. In a courtyard we tethered our horses and then sat down to one of those incomparable French meals.

It was splendid after canned stuff, and you couldn't hear the boom of a single gun. The peace of the place got hold of us—we didn't want to go back too hurriedly, and kept postponing and postponing. A blue and gold haze with a touch of silver shining through it was blurring all the sky, when we remounted. We travelled slowly, singing—thinking up the twilight songs of other times.

My thoughts went back to Scotch holidays at Arran and Loch Katrine—the daringly late evenings of childhood. Reluctantly we came back and saw the frantic city of Very lights grow up, which indicate the Hun front. The air began to be shaken again by the prolonged agony of rushing shells and stamping guns. It was only after midnight, when we had reached our hut, that I remembered the need of sleep.

But when I struck a match on entering, I found letters from each one of you awaiting—so lay late in bed reading them by candlelight for another hour. One snatches at small pleasures and magnifies them into intensity.

Your letters told me about *Carry On* and seeing "Colonel Newcome," and about the Highlanders in New York. What a very much more homely place America must be to you now. I must say I am keen to see the book. It's not mine at all—it's you dear home people's—you called it out and you put it together.

Here I sit in the underground place which I have to call "home" at present. You go through all kinds of contortions to enter. Leacock could be very funny at my expense.

7

France
June 2, 1917

It is 11 a.m., and I'm sitting at the bottom of a dugout waiting for the Hun to finish his morning hate before I go upstairs. He seems very angry and has just caved in one of our walls.

Mother seemed most awfully sorry for me in her last letter. But you know I'm really having rather a good time, despite having a minimum amount of washing and having our mess kitchen blown in every few days. The only time that one gets melancholy is when nothing is doing. An attack or the preparations for an attack are real fun. Everybody is on his toes and there's no time to think.

It's four hours later. Just as I had reached this point news came that some of our chaps were buried, so I had a little brisk spade-work, then a wriggling voyage through a hole, and then a lot of messy work pouring iodine into wounds and binding up. I'm afraid my hands are still rather like a murderer's. Incidentally our kitchen is entirely done for this time. We've got the wounded fellows on their way to Blighty and are fairly confident that they're not going west this time.

I am so glad that the coming of America into the game has made so much difference to you. I wish I could come back for a fortnight and share the excitement with you. It's difficult to picture New York as a military pageant in khaki. Tell me all about the young fellows I know and what they are doing. I wonder how many are in the field artillery—which is about the most interesting part of the game.

You remember that calvary I told you about. I saw it under another guise after writing. Something happened and, instead of the spring peace, it was a shamble with horses and men dying. In such cases one can't do anything he has to go on about his own errand. I'm so very dirty that I'll leave off now while there's a chance to have a wash. I'm awfully muddy, and my hair is just ready for growing potatoes there's about a pound of the real estate of France in it.

8

France
June 6, 1917

You certainly are owed a whole lot of letters, but it is very difficult to find the time under present conditions—I didn't get my breakfast until 7.30 p.m. yesterday. And today I was up at 4 a.m., and didn't come back from up front till dusk. So you see I really have some excuse for being temporarily a bad correspondent. You don't need to be sorry for me though, or anything like that, for I'm having quite a good time. After the mud this hard white sunlight is a God-send. Do you remember—

June 7th. Thus far I got when I was interrupted and another day has gone by. I'm just back again from up front. I went there at dawn to do some reconnaissance work. By eight the heat was sweltering just the way it was when we made our memorable trip down the Loire Valley—only now there are no estaminets at which to drink Giro Citron. The only inhabitants of the place where I am now are the mayor and his daughter, who returned the moment the town was captured. Rather fine of them. Yesterday a French soldier looked in (on special leave) to claim what was left of his cottage; just as much, I should imagine, as you could make into a road. And yet, despite the fallen houses, the fruit-trees are green and not so long ago were white with bloom and nodding.

I'm feeling extraordinarily lazy and comfortable. I've taken two hours over shaving and washing. My basin was the brass case of a big eight-inch naval shell which was formerly the property of the Hun. I wish I could send you one back. Two mornings ago I had a dive and swim in a shell-hole filled with rain-water, which gives you some idea of the sized crater a big shell can make.

From henceforth, however, I shall have to eschew this pleasure, as I understand that the ground is so poisoned with corpses, etc. ,that the water is likely to bring on skin disease. I have that to a slight extent already. Most of us have it—comes from eating no vegetables and nothing but tinned stuff.

How interested you'd be if you could just go for a couple of hours' walk with me. Coming back today I marvelled that we had ever managed to make our advance; the Hun machine-gun emplacements were so strongly fortified and well-chosen. It speaks volumes for the impetuosity of our infantry.

9

France
June 17, 1917

I believe it must be nearly a week since I wrote. The reason is that I'm down at the wagon-lines, supposed to be resting, which is when we work the hardest. First of all we had a grand inspection of the brigade, which kept one going from 5 a.m. to 10.30 p.m., cleaning harness. Then we had brigade sports, which are not yet over and which don't leave an officer with any leisure. The best time for letter-writing is when one is in action, since you sit in a dugout for interminable hours with nothing much to keep you busy.

I'm looking forward very much to the receipt of *Carry On*; it hasn't come yet. It will be like reading something absolutely beyond my knowledge.

It is now evening. This has been a mixed day. I've been orderly officer. This morning I heard Canon Scott preach—he was the father I wrote to you about whom I met going up front in the winter to look for the body of his son. He's a fine old chap and fully believes that he's fated to leave his bones in France. This afternoon was spent in harness-cleaning and this evening in watching a brigade display of boxing. A strange world! But you'll judge that we're having quite good times.

Last night we had an open-air concert—*Silver Threads Among the Gold, The Long Long Trail,* etc. Trenches lay behind us and ahead of us—not so long ago Huns could have reached us with a revolver shot, where we were all sitting. Overhead, like rooks through twilight, our righting planes sailed home to bed. Far away on the horizon, observers in the Hun balloons must have been watching us. It was almost possible to forget that a war existed; almost, until a reminder came with a roar and column of black smoke to a distant flank.

Monday. This letter gets scribbled in pieces. I'm now waiting for the afternoon parade to fall in. The gramophone is strumming out a banjo song, and in my galvanised hut it's as hot as———.Most of the men strip off everything but their breeches and go about their horses dripping like stokers. The place isn't so unlike Petewawa in some respects, except that there is no water. You look for miles across a landscape of sage-green and chalk, with straight French roads running without a waver from skyline to skyline. There's nothing habitable in sight—only gray piles and splintered trees. But in spite of the wholesale destruction one finds beauty.

You'd smile if you could see our camp—it looks like a collection of gipsy bivouacs made of lean-tos of wood with canvas and sand-bags for roofs. The rats are getting bold and coming out of the trenches—rather a nuisance. It's strange to be here playing football on the very ground over which not so long ago I followed the infantry within half an hour of the commencement of the attack. Our wounded chaps were crawling back, trying to drag themselves out of the Hun barrage, which was ploughing up the ground all around, and the Huns were lying like piled up wheat sacks in their battered front-line.

One learns to have a very short memory and to be glad of the present. Within sight a little trench tramway runs just like the Welsh toy-railway of our childhood. It leads all the way to Blighty and New York and Kootenay. One can see the wounded coming out on it, and sometimes sees them with a little envy.

10

France
June 23, 1917

Last night *Carry On* arrived. I found the officers' mess assembled round my mail—they'd guessed what was in the package. I had intended smuggling the book away and did actually succeed in getting it into my trench-coat pocket. A free fight ensued and, since there were four against one, I was soon conquered. Then one of them, having taken possession of the little volume, danced about our tin tabernacle reading extracts.

I had planned to ride into a neighbouring city for dinner that night, but sat reading till nearly twelve. Papa's preface is most beautiful and I am entirely unworthy of it. I can't thank you all enough for your loving work. I think the proof of how well you have done it is that my brother officers are quite uncynically keen about it.

If they, who have shared the atmosphere which I have unconsciously set down in its pages, can read with eagerness and without ridicule, I think the book, as compiled by you dear people, should stand the test. It's a queer little intimate peep into our family affections, almost too intimate and sacred for publication. It's a glimpse that makes me proud of all of you. So proud!

Do you remember a description I gave you some months back of seeing Huns brought up from a captured dugout? That's long enough ago now for me to be able to give you a few details. A fortnight before the show commenced it was planned that an officer from each battery with a party of volunteers should follow up the infantry attack and build a road through the Hun front-line over which our artillery should advance. The initial work was carried on at night and the road was built right up to our own front-line.

On the morning of the attack I took my volunteers forward and hid with the rest of the party in one of our support trenches. We judged that we should escape the Hun barrage there and should have advanced before his retaliation on our back-country commenced.

Soon after midnight, on a cold morning when the sleet was falling, we set out. The sky was faintly tinged with a gray dawn when our offensive opened. Suddenly the intense and almost spiritual quiet was changed into frantic chaos.

The sky was vividly lit with every kind of ingeniously contrived destruction. In addition to his other shells, the Hun flung back gas and liquid fire. It looked as though no infantry could live in it. Within an hour of the offensive starting, each officer crept out of his trench and went forward to reconnoitre the ground, taking with him one N.C.O. and a runner. My runner carried with him a lot of stakes with white rags attached for marking out our route.

We wound our way carefully through the shells until we reached our own front-line. Here the Hun barrage was falling briskly and gas-shells were coming over to beat the band. The bursting of explosives was for all the world like corn popping in a pan. We ran across what had been No Man's Land and entered the Hun wire. My job was to build from here to his support-trenches. His front-line trench was piled high with dead.

The whole spectacle was unreal as something that had been staged; the corpses looked like waxworks. One didn't have time to observe much, for flames seemed to be going off beneath one's feet almost every second and it seemed marvellous that we contrived to live where there was so much death. As we went further back we began to find our own khaki-clad dead. I don't think the Huns had got them; it was our own barrage, which they had followed too quickly in the eagerness of the attack.

Then we came to where the liquid fire had descended, for the poor fellows had thrown themselves into the pools in the shell-holes and only the faces and arms were sticking out. Then I recognised the support-trench, which was the end of my journey, and planted my Union Jack as a signal for the other officers who were to build ahead of me. With my runner and N.C.O.I started to reconnoitre my road back, planting my stakes to mark the route.

When I was again at what had been our front-line, I sent my runner back to guide in my volunteers. What a day it was! For a good part of the time the men had to dig, wearing their gas-helmets. You never saw such a mess—sleet driving in our faces, the ground hissing and boiling as shells descended, dead men everywhere, the wounded crawling desperately, dragging themselves to safety. I saw sights of pity and bravery that it is best not to mention, and all the time my brave chaps dug on, making the road for the guns.

Soon through the smoke gray-clad figures came in tottering droves, scorched, battered, absolutely stunned. They looked more like beasts in their pathetic dumbness. One hardly recognised them as enemies.

All day we worked, not stopping to eat, and by the evening we saw the first of our guns advancing. It's a great game, this war, and searches the soul out. That night I slept in the mud, clothes and all, the dreamless sleep of the dog-tired.

Note: Lieutenant Coningsby Dawson was wounded in the right arm at Vimy on June 26. He was evacuated with a serious case of gas-gangrene, and after being in first a casualty clearing hospital and then a base hospital, was sent back to England on July 8th, where he was in a hospital at Wandsworth, London, till the end of August. His arm was in such a serious condition that at first it was thought necessary to amputate it. Fortunately after days of ceaseless care this was avoided.

11

Hospital
London
July 8, 1917

A fortnight ago today I got wounded. The place was stitched up and didn't look bad enough to go out with. Three days later there was an attack and I was to be observer. My arm got poisoned while I was on the job and when I came back I was sent out. Bloodpoisoning started and they had to operate three times; for a little while there was a talk of amputation. But you're not to worry at all about me now, for I'm getting on splendidly and there's no cause for anxiety.

They tell me it will take about two months before I get the full use of my arm back. Reggie was in London on leave and got his leave extended—I missed him by an hour. J. L. Was round to see me this morning and is cabling to you. I don't think you ought to cross while the risk is so great and there's a difficulty in obtaining passports—though you know how I'd love to have you. How goes the book? I've missed all my letters for the past fortnight. Please excuse me, for my arm gets very tired, and I'm not supposed to use it.

12

London
July 25, 1917

I'm going on all right, but can't use my arm much for writing just at present, so you won't mind short letters, will you? I got the first written by you since I was hurt, yesterday. I am so glad that America is so patriotic.

Yesterday, to my great surprise, I was called up by the High Commissioner of Canada, and ongoing to see him found that he wanted me to start at once on preparing an important government statement. Since I'm forbidden to use my arm for writing, I'm to have a stenographer and dictate my stuff after doing the interviewing. This job is only temporary. And I think it is possible after I have finished it, if they refuse to allow me to return to the Front at once, that I may get a leave to America. I wouldn't want to get a long one as I am so anxious to get back to France.

Don't worry at all about me. I feel quite well now, and go about with my arm in a sling and am allowed out of hospital to do this work all day. As soon as my arm grows stronger I'll write you a good long letter, but while it is as it is at present I have to restrict myself to bare essentials.

O, did I tell you? I wouldn't have missed coming through London on a stretcher for pounds. The flower-girls climbed into the ambulance and showered us with roses. All the way as we passed people waved and shouted. It was a kind of royal procession, and, like a baby, I cried.

13

London
August 3, 1917

I've just come back to my office in Oxford Circus from

lunching at the Rendezvous. Next to my table during lunch were two typical Wardour Street dealers, rubbing their hands and chortling over a cheap buy.

I wonder how long this different way of life is going to last. Someone will snap his fingers and heigh-ho, presto! I shall be back in France. This little taste of the old life gives me a very vivid idea of the sheer glee with which I shall greet the end of the war.

How jolly comfortable it will be to be your own master not that one ever is his own master—while there are other people to live for. But I mean what an extraordinary miracle it will seem to be allowed to reckon one's life in years and not in weeks—to be able to look forward and plan and build.

And yet—this is a confession—I can see myself getting up from my easy-chair and going out again quite gladly directly there is another war, if my help is needed. There was a time, long ago, when I used to regard a soldier with horror and wondered how decent folk could admire him; the red of his coat always seemed to me the blood-red of murder. But it isn't the killing that counts—you find that out when you've become a soldier; it's the power to endure and walk bravely, and the opportunity for dying in a noble way.

One doesn't hate his enemy if he's a good soldier and doesn't even want to kill him from any personal motive he may even regret killing him while in the act. I think it's just this attitude that makes our Canadians so terrible—they kill from principle and not from malice.

I'm seeing all my old friends again, lunching with one and dining with another, and have been to some matinees. But I can go to no evening performances, because I have to be in the hospital at 10 p.m.

I really am hoping to get a week in New York after this piece of work is done, after which back to France till the war is ended.

14

London
August 30, 1917

I've just left hospital and am staying at this hotel. You keep saying in your letters that you never heard how I got my injury. I described it—but that letter must have gone astray.

On June 26th I was wounded not by a shell, but by a piece of an iron chimney which was knocked down onto my right arm. I had it sewn up and for two days it was all right. The third I went up for an attack and it started to swell—by the time I came back I had gas-gangrene. The arm is better now and I'm on sick leave, though still working.

They've made me an offer of a job here in London, but I should break my heart if I could not go back to the Front. But I think when I've finished here that I may get a special leave with permission to call in at New York. Wouldn't that be grand? I don't want to raise your hopes too high, but it seems extremely likely that I shall see you shortly. I was today before my medical board, and they gave me two months home service. I have been promised that as soon as a new Canadian ruling on home leave is confirmed, my application for leave will go through.

If that happens, I shall cable you at once that I am coming. It doesn't seem at all possible or true that this can be so and I'm making myself no promises till I'm really on the boat. It would be better that you should not, also. I'm taking a gamble and am going to order a new tunic for the occasion this afternoon.

It's a golden afternoon outside—the kind that turns the leaves red at Kootenay, with the tang of iced wine in the air. The sound of London is like the tumming of a thousand banjos. It's good to be alive and very wonderful after all that has happened.

Note: Lieutenant Coningsby Dawson arrived at Quebec on September 26th and came home on the following day. He was at home for a month. During that time he spoke in public on several occasions, and wrote the book which was brought out the following spring, entitled The Glory of the Trenches.

15

Somewhere on the Atlantic
November 11, 1917

Here's the first letter since I left New York, coming to you. It's seven in the morning; I'm lying in my bunk, expecting any minute to be called to my bath.

So far it's been a pleasant voyage, with rolling seas and no submarines. There are scarcely a hundred passengers, of whom only four are ladies, in the first class. The men are Government officials, army and navy officers going on Cook's Tours, and Naval attaches. The American naval men are an especially fine type. We do all the usual things—play cards, deck-golf and sleep immoderately, but always at the wrong times.

I'm going back for the second time and going back in the most placid frame of mind. I compare this trip with my first trip over as a soldier. I was awfully anxious then, and kept saying goodbye to things for the last time. Now I live day by day in a manner which is so take-it-for-granted as to be almost commonplace. I've locked my imagination away in some garret of my mind and the house of my thoughts is very quiet.

What bricks you all were in the parting—there wasn't any whining—you were a real soldier's family and I felt proud of you. It was just a kind of "Good luck, old chap"—with all the rest of the speaking left to the eyes and hands. That's the way it should be in a world that's so full of surprises.

This trip has done a tremendous lot for me—I shall always know now that the trenches are not the whole of the horizon. Before, when I landed in France, it seemed as though a sound and sight-proof curtain had dropped behind and everything I had known and loved was at an end. One collects a little bit of shrapnel and, heigho, presto! one's home again. On my second trip, the war won't seem such a world without end.

Tonight I have to pack—that's wonderful, too. I'm wondering whether Reggie will be on the station. I shall send a telegram to warn him.

16

This was the date at which I had to report back at headquarters. Actually I reported back yesterday because today is Sunday. I found that I had been detailed not for France, but for work under the High Commissioner. You know what such news means to me. I at once did my best to fight the order, but was told that it was a military order in which I had no choice. I start work tomorrow at Oxford Circus House, but shall put in an urgent request to go to France.

I shall at least try to get some limitations to the period of my stay in England. Even when I was in hospital I used to feel that the last stretcher-case out of the fighting was someone to be worshipped he was nearer to the sacrifice than I. And now I'm not to go back for months, perhaps—I shall eat my heart out in England.

Reggie fell asleep and has just wakened. He was dreaming, he said, the best dream in the world. It was that he might land back in New York on December 20th and spend Christmas with you—then go up to Kootenay to get a glimpse of his little green home among the snow and apple trees and—"And then what?" I asked.

He made a wry face. "Go back to hunting submarines," he said quickly. Go back! We all want to go back. Why? Because it's so easy to find reasons for not going back probably. I shall raise heaven and earth to be sent back—and you'll be glad of it.

There's something that I shouldn't tell you were I going back tomorrow. Last week I met one of my gunners on leave. He was standing on the island in Piccadilly Circus. I learnt from him that every officer who was with me at the battery when I was wounded has since been wiped out. Even some who joined since have been done for. Three have been killed, the rest wounded, gassed, and the major has gone out with concussion.

Among the killed is poor S., the one who was my best friend in France. You remember he had a young wife and his first baby was born in February. He used to carry the list of all the people I wanted written to if I were killed, and I had promised to do the same for him. In addition to the officers, many of the men whom I admired have "gone west."

All this was told me casually in the heart of London's pleasure with the taxis and busses streaming by.

A few days ago a pitiful derelict of the streets crossed my path. I'd been dining out in the West End with L. and P. and was on my way back, when a girl stopped me. She stopped me for the usual reason, and I suppose I refused her rudely. The next thing I knew she was crying. She said she had been walking for twelve hours, and was cold and tired, and ready to fall from weariness. It was very late and I scarcely knew where to take her, but we found a little French restaurant open in Gerrard Street.

On coming into the light, I discovered that she had a little toy dog under her arm, just as tired of life as herself. It was significant that she attended to the dog's before her own needs. We had to tempt it with milk before it would eat—then she set to work herself ravenously.

I learnt her story by bits. She was a discharged munition worker, had strained herself lifting shells and hadn't the brains or strength for anything but the streets. When she left the restaurant the lap-dog was again tucked beneath her arm. It was nearly midnight when she disappeared in the raw chilliness of the scant electric light. People die worse deaths than on battle-fields.

Wednesday. I've been working for the last three days at the Minister's, and still have no inkling of what is to happen to me. My major walked in today; he wants me to wait till his sick-leave is over, after which we can return together. He'll put in a strong personal request for me to be allowed to return. He got concussion of the brain eight weeks ago through a shell bursting in his dug-out.

S. was wounded at the same time, but didn't go out till next day. He had got 100 yards from the battery when he and his batman were killed instantly by the same shell.

Reggie wasn't in town when I arrived. He didn't meet me

till Friday. What with playing with him and working here I don't get much time for writing. But you'll hear from me again quite soon.

17

The Ritz, London
November 15, 1917

This hanging round London seems a very poor way to help win a war. I couldn't stand very much of it, however invaluable they pretended I was, when my pals are dying out there. Poor old S.! He's in my thoughts every hour of the day. He was always getting new photos of his little daughter. He longed for a Blighty that he might see her again. He was wounded, but stopped on duty for two days. At last, only one hundred yards down the trench on his way to the dressing-station a shell caught him. He was dead in an instant.

Before the Vimy show two of our chaps in the mess had peculiar dreams: one saw D.'s grave and the other S.'s. Both S. and D. are dead. The effect that all this has on me is not what might be expected—makes me the more anxious to get back. I hate to think that others are going sleepless and cold and are in danger, and that I am not there. When the memory comes at meal-times I feel like leaving the table. Of course I'm an ass; I shall get out soon enough. When I do get out, I shall know just how great an ass I am at this moment. In the army the sensible game is to accept all the pleasantness that one can get in the present—there's plenty of the other stuff.

It was ripping to hear from you last night. Your letter greeted me as I returned from the theatre. We'd been out with my major. At the theatre we picked up with a plucky chap, named K., who belonged to the same battery as B., to whom, you remember, I was carrying a present from some girl in New York.

The present which she was so keen should reach him by Christmas turned out to be a necktie which she had knitted for him. On asking K., I found out that B. was killed on October 31st. It's the same story all the time so far as the 18-pounders are concerned.

When Reggie leaves me I'm going to start on another book, *Out to Win*, which is to be an interpretation for England of the new spirit which is animating America, and a plea for a closer sense of kinship between my two nations.

Don't worry about me, you'll get a cabled warning before I go to France. My major expects to go back in a month or two, and we've arranged to return together if possible. But you needn't get worried—I'm afraid I shall probably spend Christmas in London.

18

The Ritz, London
November 17, 1917

Your minds can be at rest as regards my safety for a few weeks at least. I've been collared for fair, but I think I'll manage to get free again presently. I suppose you'll say that I'm a donkey to want so much to get back to the front; perhaps I am the war will last quite long enough for every man in khaki to get very much more of it than he can comfortably stomach. The proper soldierly attitude is to take every respite as it turns up and be grateful for it.

But then I'm not a professional soldier. I think in saying that I've laid my finger on the entire reason for the splendour of our troops that they're not professional soldiers, but civilian idealists. Your professional soldier isn't particularly keen on death—his game is to live that he may fight another day. Our game is to fight and fight and fight so long as we have an ounce of strength left. My major and myself are all that are left of the officers in my battery. A great many of our best men are gone. They need us back to help them out.

Here's a story of stories—one which answers all the questions one hears asked as to whether the army doesn't lower a man's morals and turn saints into blackguards.

When we were on the Somme, a batch of very worthless-appearing remounts arrived at our wagon-lines direct from

England. When they were paraded before us, they made the rottenest impression—they looked like molly-coddles whom the army had cowed.

Among them was a particularly inoffensive-looking young man who had been a dental student, whom, if the Huns could have seen him as a sample of the kind of reinforcements we were getting, they would certainly have taken new courage to win the war. All the officers growled and prayed God for a consignment of the old rough-and-tumble knockabout chaps who came out of gaols, from under freight-trains and from lumber-camps to die like gentlemen the only gentlemanly thing they ever did, I expect—with the Canadian First Contingent.

A few weeks later we sent back to the wagon-lines for a servant to be sent up to the guns, two of our batmen having been killed and a third having been returned to duty. The wagon-line officer sent us up this fellow with the following note: "I'm sending you X. He's the most useless chap I have—not bad, but a ninny. I hope he'll suit you."

He didn't. He could never carry out an order correctly and seemed scared stiff by any N.C.O. or officer. We got rid of him promptly. When he returned to the wagon-lines, he was put on to all the fatigues and dirty jobs.

The first time we got any hint that the chap had guts was when we were out at rest at Christmas. He'd been shifted from one section to another, because no one wanted him. Each new Number One as he received him put him on to his worst horses, so as to get rid of him the more quickly. The chap was grooming a very ticklish mare, when she up with her hind-legs and caught him in the chest, throwing him about twenty yards into the mud. He lay stunned for a full minute; we thought he was done.

Then, in a dazed kind of way, he got upon his feet. He was told he could fall out, but he insisted upon finishing the grooming of his horse. When the stable parade was dismissed, much against his will he was sent to be inspected by the brigade doctor.

The doctor looked him over and said, "I ought to send you out to a hospital, but I'll see how you are tomorrow. You must go back to your billets and keep quiet. The kick has chipped the point of your breast-bone."

"It didn't," said Driver X, "and I'm not going to lie down."

The doctor, who is very small, looked as much like the Last Judgement as his size would allow. "You'll do what you're told," he said sharply. "You'll find yourself up for office if you speak to me like that. If I told you that both your legs were broken, they would be broken. You don't know very much about the army, my lad."

"But my breast-bone isn't chipped," he insisted. Contrary to orders he was out on the afternoon parade and was up to morning stables next day at six o'clock. When strafed for his disobedience, he looked mild and inoffensive and obstinate. He refused to be considered, and won out. You can punish chaps for things like that; but you don't.

The next thing we noticed about him was that he was learning to swear. Then he began to look rough, so that no one would have guessed that he came from a social grade different from that of the other men. And this was the stage he had arrived at when I got wounded last summer and left the battery. The story of his further progress was completed for me this week when I met my major in town.

"Who's the latest hero, do you think?" he questioned. "You'd never guess—the dental student. He did one of the most splendid bits of work that was ever done by an artillery driver."

Here's what he did. He was sent along a heavily shelled road at nightfall to collect material from blown-in dugouts for building our new battery position. He was wheel-driver on a G.S. wagon which had three teams hooked into it. There was a party of men with him to scout up the material and an N.C.O. in charge.

As they were halted, backed up against an embankment, a shell landed plumb into the wagon, crippling it badly, wounding all the horses and every man except the ex-dental student.

The teams bolted and it was mainly due to the efforts of the wheel-driver that the stampede was checked. He must have used quite a lot of language which really polite people would not have approved. He then bound up all the wounds of his comrades—there was no one to help him and took them back to the field dressing-station two at a time, mounted on two of the least wounded horses. When he had carried them all to safety, he removed their *puttees* and went back alone along the shelled road to the wounded horses and used the *puttees* to stop their flow of blood. He managed to get the wagon clear, so that it could be pulled. He tied four of the horses on behind; hooked in the two that were strongest, and brought the lot back to the wagon-lines single-handed.

And here's the end of the story. The O.C. put in a strong recommendation that he be decorated for his humanity and courage. The award came through in the record time of fourteen days, with about a yard of military medal ribbon and congratulations from high officers all along the line. The morning of the day it came through thieving had been discovered in the battery, and a warning had been read out that the culprit was suspected and that it would go hard with him when he was arrested. The decoration was received in the afternoon while harness-cleaning was in progress.

Without loss of time the O.C. went out, a very stern look on his face, and had the battery formed up in a hollow square. There was only one thought in the men's heads—that the thief had been found. There was a kind of "Is it I" look in their faces. Without explanation, the O.C. called upon the ex-dental student to fall out. He fell out with his knees knocking and his chin wobbling, looking quite the guilty party. Then the O.C. commenced to read all the praise from officers at brigade, division, corps, army, of the gallant wheel-driver who had not only risked his life to save his pals, but had even had the fineness of fore-thought to bind up the horses' wounds with the *puttees*.

Then came the yard of military medal ribbon, a piece of which was snipped off and pinned onto the lad's worn tunic.

The battery yelled itself crimson. The dental student had learnt to swear, but he'd won his spurs. He's been promoted to the most dangerous and coveted job for a gunner or driver in the artillery; he's been put onto the B.C. party, which has to go forward into all the warm spots to observe the enemy and to lay in wire with the infantry when a "show" is in progress. Can you wonder that I get weary of seeing the London busses trundle along the well-swept asphalt of Oxford Street and long to take my chance once more with such chaps?

19

London
November 29, 1917

Here's such a November London day as no American ever imagines. A feeling of spring and greenness is in the air, and a glint of subdued gold. This morning as I came across Battersea Bridge it seemed as though war could not be—that, at worst, it was only an incident. The river lay below me so old and good-humoured—in front Cheyne Walk comfortably ancient and asleep. Through the chimneys and spires of the distant city blue scarfs of mist twisted and floated.

Everything looked very happy. Boys—juvenile cannon-fodder went whistling along the streets; housemaids leant shyly out of upstairs windows, shaking dusters to attract their attention. In the square by the Chelsea Pensioners, soldiers, all spit and polish, were going through their foot-drill; they didn't look too earnest about it—not at all as if in two months they would be in the trenches. It's the same with the men on leave—they live their four-teen days with cheery commonsense as though they were going to live forever.

It's impossible, even when you meet the wounded, to discover any sign of tragedy in London. The war is referred to as "good old war," "a bean feast," "a pretty little scrap," but never as an undertaking of blood and torture. Last night there was strong moonlight, very favourable to an air-raid. When I bought my paper this morning, the fat woman, all burst out and tied in at the most unexpected places, remarked to me with an air of disappointment,

"They fergot h'us."

"Who forgot us?" I asked.

"The bloomin' 'Uns. I wus h'expecting them lawst night."

She spoke as though she'd had tea ready and the kettle boiling for a dear friend who had misremembered his engagement. England has set out to behave as if there was no death; she's jolly nearly succeeded in eliminating it from her thoughts. She's learnt the lesson from the chaps in the front-line trenches, and she's like a mother—like our mother—who has sons at the war—she's going to keep on smiling so as not to let her fellows down.

All the streets are full of girls in khaki—girls with the neatest, trimmest little ankles. The smartest of all are the Flying Corps girls, many of whom drive the army cars in the most daring manner. When you think of what they are and were, the war hasn't done so badly for them. They were purposeless before. Their whole aim was to get married. They felt that they weren't wanted in the world. They broke windows with Mother Pankhurst. Now they've learnt discipline and duty and courage. They'd man the trenches if we'd let them.

They used to sneer at our sex; whether they married or remained single, quite a number of them became man-haters. But now—that kind of civil war is ended. Ask the young subaltern back on leave how much he is disliked by the girls. Babies and home have become the fashion. I received quite a shock last Sunday when I was saluted by one of these girls—saluted in a perfectly correct and soldierly fashion.

The idea is right; if they outwardly acknowledge that they are a part of the army, military discipline becomes their protection. But what a queer, changed world from the world of sloppy blouses, cheap and much-too-frequent jewellery, and silly sentimental ogling! England's become more alert and forthright; despite the war, she's happier.

This isn't meant for a glorification of war; it's simply a statement of fact. The time had to come when women would be-come men; they've become men in this most noble and wom-anly fashion—through service. They're doing men's jobs with women's alacrity.

There is only one thing that will keep me from rejoining my battery in January, and that's this American book. We have come to the conclusion that to complete the picture of American de-termination to win out, I ought to go on a tour of inspection in France. The Government is interested in the book for propa-ganda work. The extreme worthwhileness of such an undertak-ing would reconcile me to a postponement of my return to the Front—nothing else will.

All the papers here are full of the details of the advance at Cambrai. I want to be "out there," so badly. What does it matter that there's mud in the trenches, and death round every traverse, and danger in each step? It's the hour of glorious life I long for; for such an hour I would exchange all the sheeted beds and run-ning bath-taps, not to mention the *aeons* of Cathay.

I can see those gunners forcing up their guns through the mire and can hear the machine-guns clicking away like infuri-ated typewriters. The whole gigantic pageant of death and en-deavour moves before me—and I'm sick of clubs and safety. People say to me, "You're of more use here—you can serve your country better by being in England."

But when chaps are dying I want to take my chance with them. Don't be afraid I'll be kept here. I won't. I didn't know till I was held back against my will what a grip that curious existence at the Front had got on me. It isn't the horror one remembers—it's the exhilaration of the glory.

Cheer up, I'll be home some Christmas to fill your Christmas stocking. It won't be this Christmas perhaps not the next; but perhaps the next after that. The young gentlemen from the navy will be there too to help me. It's a promise.

I was present at the opening of the American Officers' Club by the Duke of Connaught. This club is the private house of Lord Leconfield. Other people have presented furniture, pictures and money. It costs an American officer next to nothing, and is the best attempt that has been made to give a welcome to the U.S.A. in London. It's the most luxurious club in the West End at present.

20

London
December 10, 1917

I got a letter from the Foreign Office, asking me to go back to America to do writing and lecturing for the British Mission. I'm sure you'll appreciate why I refused it, and be glad. I couldn't come back to U.S.A. to talk about nobilities when their sons and brothers are getting their first baptism of fire in the trenches. If I'd got anything worth saying I ought to be out there in the mud,—saying it in deeds. But I've told Colonel B. that if ever I come out again wounded I will join the British Mission for a time. So now you have something to look forward to.

I hear though that permission will probably be granted to me within the next few days to start for France to go through the American lines and activities. You can guess how interesting that will be to me. I only hope they have a fight on while I'm in the American lines.

I suppose the tour will take me the best part of a month, so I'll be away from England for Christmas. I rather hope I'll be in Paris—ever since reading *Trilby* I've longed to go to the Madeleine for Noël—which reminds me that I must get *Trilby* to read on the journey. It's rather a romantic life that I'm having nowadays, don't you think? I romp all over the globe and, in the intervals, have a crack at the Germans. After I have finished writing this book on the American activities in France I shan't be content a moment till I've rejoined my battery. I feel a terrible shyster stopping away from the fighting a day longer than can be helped. This book, which I intend to be a spiritual interpretation of the soul of America, ought to do good to Anglo-American relations; so it seems of sufficiently vital importance.

I can't think of anything that would do more to justify the

blotting out of so many young lives than that, when the war is ended, England and America should have reason to forget the last hundred and thirty years of history, joining hands in a world-wide Anglo-Saxon alliance against the future murdering of nations. If I can contribute anything towards bringing that about, the missing of two months in the trenches will be worth it.

I went to a "good luck" dinner the other night, which we gave to my major on the occasion of his setting sail for Canada. Two others of the officers who used to be with me in the battery are to be on the same ship. A year ago in the Somme we used to pray for a blighty today, every officer in our mess has either got a blighty or is dead. It gives one some idea of the brevity of our glory.

You'd love the West End shops were you here. I've just drawn down my blinds on Oxford Street; I walked back by way of Regent Street after lunch—all the windows are gay and full. Men in khaki are punting their girls through the crowds, doing their Christmas shopping. You can see the excited faces of little children everywhere. There doesn't seem to be much hint of war.

One wonders whether people are brave to smile so much or only careless. You hear of tremendous lists of casualties, but there are just as many men. It looks as though we had man-power and resources to carry on the war interminably. There's only one class of person who is fed up—and that's the person who has done least sacrificing. The person who has done none at all is a nervous wreck and can't stand the strain much longer. But ask the fighting men—they're perfectly happy and contented. Curious! When you've given everything, you can always give some more.

This may reach you before Christmas, though I doubt it. If it does, be as merry as we shall be, though absent.

21

London
December 10, 1917
I hope you feel as I do about my refusal of Colonel B.'s offer

to send me back to America on the British Mission. I was also approached today to do press work for the Canadians. It seems as though everyone was conspiring to throw tempting plums in my way to keep me from returning to the front.

I don't know that I'm much good as a soldier; probably I'm very much better as a writer, but it's as though my soul, my decency, my honour were at stake—I must get back to the Front. The war is going to be won by men who go back to the trenches in the face of reason and commonsense. If I had a leg off, I should try for the Flying Corps.

I may be a fool in the Front Line, but I won't be finished as a fighting man till I'm done. They can keep all their cushy jobs for other chaps—I want the mud and the pounding of the guns.

It doesn't really matter if one does get killed, provided he's set a good example. Do you remember that sermon we heard Dr. Jowett give about St. Paul at Lystra, going back after they had stoned him?

"Back to the stones"—that expresses me exactly. I hate shellfire and discomfort and death as much as any other man. But I'd rather lose everything than have to say goodbye to my standard of heroism.

I don't want to kill Huns particularly, but I do want to prove to them that we're the better men. I can't do that by going through oratorical gymnastics in America or by writing racy descriptions of the Canadians' bravery for the international press. I shall be less than nothing when I return to France—a mere subaltern whose life isn't very highly valued. But in my heart I shall know myself a man.

There's no one understands my motive but you three, who have most to lose by my cripplement or death. All my friends over here think me an ass to throw away such chances—they say I'm economically squandering myself in the place where I'm least trained to do the best work. I know they talk sense; but they don't talk chivalry. If every man took the first chance offered him to get out of the catastrophe, where would the Huns' offensive end?

You've probably been writing hard at *The Father of a Soldier*, and saying all that you would like to say to me in that. I'm most anxious to see the manuscript of it. If you please, how could the son of the man who wrote that book accept a cushy job?

I wonder if you've reached the point yet where you don't think that dying matters? I suspect you have. You remember what Roosevelt said after seeing his last son off, "If he comes back he'll have to explain to me the why and how."

That's the Japanese spirit—honour demands when a man returns from battle that he can give good reasons why he is not dead. Others, his friends and comrades, are dead; how does he happen to be living? In that connection I think of Charlie S., lying somewhere in the mud of Ypres, with an insignificant cross above his head. He won a dozen decorations which were not given him. He had a baby whom he had only seen once. He was my pal. Why should I live, while he is dead. I can always hear him singing in the mess in a pleasant tenor voice. We used to share our affections and our troubles. He was what the Canadians call "a white man." I can't see myself living in comfort while he is dead.

It's odd the things one remembers about a man. We got the idea in the Somme that oil on the feet would prevent them from becoming frozen. One time when Charlie was going up forward we hadn't any oil, so he used brilliantine. It smelt of violets and we made the highest of game of him. Poor old Charlie, he doesn't feel the cold now.

I'm afraid I've written a lot of rot in this letter—I've talked far too much of a host of things which are better left unsaid. But I had to I wanted to make quite certain that you wouldn't blame me for refusing safety. I've relieved myself immensely by getting all of this off my chest.

22

London
December 17, 1917
I'm waiting for Eric and, while waiting, propose to tell you

the story of my past few days. I think when you've come to the end of my account you'll agree that I've been mixing my drinks considerably with regards to the personalities whose acquaintance I have made.

On Friday evening I was invited to dinner by Lieutenant C., the American Navy man with whom I crossed in November. I met—whom do you think?—George Grossmith, Leslie Henson, Julia James, Madge Saunders and Lord Chaplin. I may say that Lord Chaplin is not a member of the Gaiety Company, though I seem to have included him.

The occasion was really the weekly dinner given by the American Officers' Club; the Gaiety Company was there to entertain. I think it is typical of England's attitude towards the American Army that people from such different walks of life should have been present to do the U.S.A. honour. Lord Chaplin is a splendid type of old-fashioned courtier with a great, kindly, bloodhound face. He had ensigns and officers of whatsoever rank brought to him, and spoke to them with the fine manly equality of the true-bred aristocrat.

It was amusing to see the breezy American boys quite unembarrassed, most of them unaware of Lord Chaplin's political eminence, exchanging views in the friendliest of fashions, while the old gentleman, keeping seated, leaning forward on his stick with one hand resting attentively on a young fellow's arm, expressed his warm appreciation of America's eagerness.

Grossmith was in the uniform our boys wear—that of a lieutenant in the R.N.V.R. Leslie Henson is now a mechanic in the motor-transport by day and a Gaiety star in the evenings. He says that it costs him much money to cure the ache which the army gives to his back but he continues to do his "bit" by day and to amuse Tommies home on leave in the evenings.

Next day, Saturday, I went down to Bath to meet Raemaekers, the Dutch cartoonist. Mr. Lane was our host. Raemaekers is a great man. On the journey I tried to picture him. I saw him as a pale-faced man, with lank black hair and a touch of the Jew about him. I rather expected to find him worn and slightly more than middle-aged, with nervous hands and hollow eyes. I reminded myself that of the world's artists, he was the only one who had risen to the sheerness of the occasion.

He expresses the conscience of the aloof cosmopolitan as regards Germany's war-methods. England, incurably good-humoured, has only Bairnsfather's comic portrayals of Old Bill to place beside this indignant Dutchman's moral hatred of Hun cruelty. From the station I went to the Bath Club; there I met not at all what I had imagined. He looks like a Frans Hals burgher, comfortable, with a high complexion, a small pointed beard, chestnut hair and searching gray eyes.

His charity of appearance belies him, for his eyes and mouth have a terrific purpose. His hands are the hands of a fighting man which crush. You would pass him in the street as unremarkable unless he looked at you—his eyes are daggers which stop you dead.

There were four of us at lunch he sat at my right and we talked like a river in flood. He's just back from America, thrilled by the American's unimpassioned, lawful thoroughness. He had found something akin to his own temperament in the nation's genius the same capacity to brush aside facetiousness in a crisis, and to attain a Hebrew prophet's faculty for hatred. One doesn't want to laugh when women lie dead in the ash-pits of Belgium. I have been with him many hours and have scarcely seen him smile—and yet his face is kindly.

As you know, the *Kaiser* had set a price upon his head. His death would mean more to the Hun than the destruction of many British divisions. He has pilloried the *Kaiser's* beastliness for all time.

When future ages want to know what the *Kaiser* said to Christ, they will find it all in the thousand Raemaekers' sketches. Traps have been laid for his capture from time to time. Submarines have been despatched with orders to take him alive. He knows what awaits him if such plans should meet with success a lingering, tortured death; consequently he travels armed and has promised his wife to blow his brains out the moment he is captured.

We talked of many things—of the Hague and H. among other things. He knew the P.'s and drew a sketch of Mr. P. on the tablecloth with his pencil. I tried to purchase the tablecloth that I might send it to America, but the club-secretary was before me.

In the afternoon I went to the railway-station and spoke with a porter who was pushing a barrow—Henry Chappel, who wrote *The Day*—the first war-poet of 1914. As luck would have it it was Saturday, the day upon which John Lane had brought out his volume of poems; it was rather pathetic to find him accepting six-penny tips on the proudest afternoon of his life. I told him how I had seen his poem pasted up in prominent places all the way from the Atlantic to the Pacific. He smiled in a patient fashion and said that he had heard about it. I under-stand that he made one hundred pounds out of this poem and gave it all to the Red Cross.

A gentleman, if you want to find one! I asked him if he didn't look forward to promotion now. He shook his head gravely he liked portering and wouldn't be much good at anything else. At parting I shook his hand; but, when I had dropped it, he touched his cap—and touched my heart in the doing of it.

On Sunday I was back in town. Eric turned up this morn-ing, looking clean and smiling, with an exceedingly glad eye. He's just the same a she always was, discontented with his job because he thinks it's too safe and trying to find one more dangerous. We're going to have a great time together, unless I get my marching orders from the Foreign Office.

I lunched with Raemaekers at Claridge's today and have just come back. He's an elemental moralist, encased in a burgher's exterior. He affects me with a sense of restrained power. One is surprised to see him eating like other men. How I wish that I could detest as he detests. And yet he has heart in plenty. He told me a story of a French battalion going out to die. The last soldier stepped out of the ranks towards his colonel, who was weeping for his men who would not come back. Flinging his arms about his commanding officer, he kissed him and said, "Do not fear, my colonel; we shall not disgrace you." He has an eye for magnanimity, that man.

23

London
December 31, 1917

This foggy London morning early your three letters from December 5th to 18th arrived. I jumped out of bed; lit the gas, retreated under the blankets and devoured them, leaning on my elbow.

This is the last day of the old year—a quaint old year it has been for all of us. I commenced it quite reconciled to the thought that it would be my last; and here I am, while poor Charlie S. and so many other fellows whom I loved are dead. It only shows how very foolish it is to anticipate trouble, for the last twelve months have been the very best and richest of my life. If I were to die now, I should feel that I had at least done something with my handful of years.

I'd like to have another glimpse of American now that in the face of reverses she has grown sterner. It's certain at last that there'll be a lot of American boys who won't come back. They're going to be real soldiers, going to go over the top and to endure all the fierce heroisms of an attack. It's cruel to say so, but it's better for America's soul that she should have her taste of battle after all the shouting.

On Saturday F. R. came to see us. He's home on leave. He and P. and I sitting down together after all the years that have intervened since we were at Oxford together! As F. expressed it, blinking through his spectacles, "Doesn't it seem silly that I should be dressed up like this and that you should be dressed like that?"

He went out in January as a second lieutenant, and returned commanding his battalion. God moves in a mysterious way, doesn't He? One can't help wondering why some should "go west" at once and others should be spared. Bob H., who was also with us at Oxford, as you will remember, lasted exactly six days.

The first day in the trenches he was wounded, but not sufficiently to go out. The sixth day he was killed. Did I tell you that
there's a nerve hospital near here crowded with nerve-shattered
babies on one floor and nerve-shattered Tommies on the next?
The babies are all dressed in red and the Tommies in the usual
hospital blue.

Each day the shell-shocked chaps go up to visit the children;
the moment the door opens and the blue figures appear, the little red crowd stretch out their arms and cry, "My soldier! My
soldier!" for each Tommy has his own particular pet. When a
child gets a nervous attack, it is often only the one particular
soldier who can do the soothing. Who'd think that men fresh
from the carnage could be so tender! And people say that war
makes men brutal. Humph!

24

A French Port
January 3, 1918

Here I am again in France and extraordinarily glad to be
here. I feel that I'm again a part of the game—I couldn't feel that
while I was in London. I landed here this morning and arrive in
Paris tonight. The crossing was one of the quietest. I know a lot
of people didn't lie down at all and still others slept with their
clothes on. Like a sensible fellow I crept into my berth at nine
p.m., and slept like a top till morning. If we'd been submarined
I shouldn't have known it.

I feel tremendously elated by the thought of this new adventure, and intend to make the most of it. As you know, nothing
would have persuaded me to delay my return to the front except
an opportunity for doing work of these dimensions. I really do
believe that I have the chance of a lifetime to do work of international importance. I want to make the Americans feel that
they have become our kinsmen through the magnitude of their
endeavour. And I want to make the British shake off their reti-
cence in applauding the magnanimity of America's enthusiasm.

It's been snowing here; but I don't feel cold because of the warmth inside me. The place where I am now is one of the pleasure-haunts which Eric and I visited together in that golden summer of long ago. Little did I think that I should be here next time in such belligerent attire and on such an errand. Life's a queer kaleidoscope. But, oh, for such another summer, with the long secure peace of July days, and the whole green world to wander! One doubts whether Eldorado will ever come again.

I see the W.A.C.K.s—the girl-soldiers of England—everywhere nowadays. A reinforcing draft crossed over with me on the steamer—high complexions and laughing faces, trim uniforms and tiny ankles. They're brave! It's a pity we can't give them a chance of just one crack at the Huns. But they have to stop behind the lines and drive lorries, and be good girls, and beat typewriters. Their little girl officers are mighty dignified. What a gallant world! I wouldn't have it otherwise.

For me the New Year is starting well. I face it in higher spirits than any of its predecessors. And well I may, for I didn't expect to be alive to greet 1918. I hope you are all just as much on the crest of the wave in your hopes and anticipations. Nothing can be worse than some of the experiences that lie behind and that's some comfort. Nothing can be more chivalrous than the opportunities which lie before us.

So here's goodbye to you from France once again.

25

Paris
January 8, 1918

Here I am in Paris, starting on my new adventure of writing the story of what the Americans are doing in the war. I left England on January 2nd, which was a Wednesday, and arrived here Thursday evening. As you know, while I was in the frontline I had very little idea of what France at war was like. One crossed from England, clambered on a military train with all the windows smashed, had a cold night journey and found himself at once among the shell-holes.

I was very keen on seeing what Paris was like; now that I've

139

seen it, it's very difficult to describe. It's very much the same as it always was—only while its atmosphere was once champagne, now it is a strong still wine. As in England, only to a greater extent, women are doing the work of men. The streets are full of the wounded—not the wounded with well-fitted artificial limbs that you see in London, but with ordinary wooden stumps, etc. Our English wounded are always gay and laughing—determined to treat the war as a humorous episode to the end. The French wounded are grave, afflicted and ordinary.

I think the Frenchman, with an emotional honesty of which we are incapable, has from the first viewed the war as a colossal calvary, and has seen it against the historic sky-line of a travailing world. Never by speech or gesture has he disguised the fact that he, as an individual, is engaged in a fore-ordained and unparalleled adventure of sacrifice. The Englishman, self-conscious of his own heroic gallantry, cloaks his fineness with pretended indifference and has succeeded in deceiving the world.

Our sportsmanship in the face of death impresses more complex nations as irreligion. So while London is outwardly gayer than ever, Paris has a stiff upper lip, a look of sternness in its eyes and very little laughter on its mouth. By nine-thirty in the evening every restaurant is closed and the streets are empty till the soldiers on leave troop out from the theatres.

As for the food, I have seen no shortage in France as yet. You can get plenty of butter and sugar, whereas in London margarine is rare and sugar is doled out. The talk of France being exhausted is all rubbish; you can feel the muscles of a great nation struggling the moment you land.

I have had a most kindly and helpful reception from the American Press division. They have realized with the usual American quickness of mind the importance of what I propose to do.

One of their officers starts out with me tonight on my first tour of military activities. It will take about five days. I then return to Paris to write up what I have seen and afterwards set out again in a new direction. If I take the proper advantage of my opportunities, I ought to get an amazingly interesting lot of material.

Saturday I was lucky enough to secure a car, and went the round of my introductions, to the British Embassy and your friends from Newark.

I've been to two theatres. The audiences were composed for the most part of soldiers on leave—American, British, Canadian, Australian, Belgian, French, with the merest sprinkling of civilians. Sunday I walked through the Luxembourg, most of the galleries of which are closed. Afterwards I walked in the gardens and watched the Parisians sliding on the ice.

For the moment they forgot they were at war, and became children. There were little boys and girls, soldiers with their sweethearts, fat old men and women, all running and pushing, and sliding and falling and chattering. I thought of Trilby with her grave kind eyes. Then I walked down the Boule Miche to Notre Dame, where women were praying for their dead.

Today Paris is under snow and again the child spirit has asserted itself. Soldiers and sailors are pelting one another with snowballs in the streets, and Jupiter continues to pluck his geese and send their feathers drifting down the sky.

This time last year I was marching into action with a temperature of 104 degrees and you were reaching London, wondering whether I was truly coming on leave. A queer year it has been; in spite of all our anticipations to the contrary, we're still alive. I wish we were to meet again this year, and we may. We know so little. As Whitcomb Riley says in complete acceptance of human fortuitousness, "No child knows when it goes to sleep."

26

Paris
January 13, 1918

About an hour ago I got into Paris from my first trip. I've been where M. and I spent our splendid summer so many years ago, only now the river is spanned with ice and the country is a gray sage colour. From what I can see the Americans are preparing as if for a war that is going to last for thirty years. America is in the war literally to her last man and her last dollar; when her hour comes to strike, she will be like a second England in the fight.

I made my tour with an officer who was with Hoover three years in Belgium, and who before that was a student in Paris. As a consequence he speaks French like a native. Every detail of my trip was arranged ahead by telephone and telegram; automobiles were waiting. There is no pretence about the American army. My rank as lieutenant is, of course, quite inadequate to the task I have undertaken. But the American high officer carries no side or swank. Having produced my credentials I am seated at the mess beside generals and allowed to ask any question, however searching.

Everyone I have met as yet is hats off to the English and the French—they go out of their way to make comparisons which are in their own disfavour and unjust to themselves. I have been making a particular study of their transport facilities and their artillery training. Both are being carried out on a magnificently thorough scale. I undertake to assert that they will have as fine artillery as can be found on the Western Front by the time they are ready. I certainly never saw such painstaking and methodical training.

As you know, the phase of the war that I am particularly interested in is the closeness of international relations that will result when the war is ended. The tightening of bonds between the French, Americans and English can be daily witnessed and felt. The Americans are loud in their praise of their French and British instructors—the instructors are equally proud of their pupils. On the street, in hotels and trains, the three races hobnob together.

I came back today with a French artillery and cavalry officer—splendid fellows. We had fought together on the Somme, we discovered, and had occupied the same Front, though at separate times, at Vimy.

The artilleryman was a young French noble and, as only no-

142

blemen can these days, had a car waiting for him at the station. He insisted on taking me to my hotel and we parted the most excellent friends.

I have two days in which to write up my experiences, and on Tuesday I shall set out on a tour in a new direction. So much I am able to tell you; the rest will be in my book when it is published.

This time last year we were together in London—how long ago it seems and sounds! Years are longer and of more value than they once were. This year I'm here. Next year where? This time next year the war will not be ended, I'm certain, nor even the year after that, perhaps. The more we feel our strength, the more we are called upon to suffer; the sterner will become our terms.

It's nearly eleven, my dear ones, and time that I was asleep. I have Henri Bordeaux's story of *The Last Days of Fort Vaux* beside me—it's most heroic reading. What shall we do when the gates of heroism grow narrow and peace has been declared? Something spiritual will have gone out of life when the challenge of the horrible is ended.

27

Paris
January 19, 1918

I'm expecting to go to American Headquarters on Tuesday and to see something of work immediately behind the lines. I find what I am doing exceptionally interesting and hope to do a good book on it.

Wherever one goes the best men one meets are Hoover's disciples from Belgium. They tell extraordinary stories of the heroism of the patriots whom they knew there people by the score who duplicated Miss Cavell's courage and paid the penalty. Their experience of Hun brutality has somehow dulled their sense of horror—they speak of it as something quite commonplace and to be expected.

On Friday I saw Miss Holt's work for the blind. She bears out for France all that I have said about the amazing sharing of the wounded in England. One man in her care was not only totally blind, but he had also lost both arms. In the hospital there were men less grievously mutilated than himself, who hardly knew how to endure their loss.

For the sake of the cheeriness of his example, he used to go round the ward with gifts of cigarettes, which he almost thought he lit for the men himself, for he used to say to Miss Holt before undertaking such a journey, "You are my hands."

We, in England, and still less in America, have never approached the loathing which is felt for the Boche in France. Men spit as they utter his name, as though the very word was foul in the mouth. Wherever you go lonely men or women are pointed out to you; all of his or her family are behind the German lines. We think we have suffered, but we have not sounded one fathom of this depth of agony.

On every hand I hear that the French army is stronger than ever, better equipped and more firm in its morale. As an impassioned Frenchman said to me yesterday, his eyes blazing as he banged the table, "They shall not pass. I say so—and I am France."

In the face of all this I do not wonder that the French misunderstand the easy good-humour with which we English go out to die. In their eyes and with the throbbing of their wounds, this war is a matter for neither good-humour nor sportsmanship, but only for the indignant, inarticulate wrath of a Hebrew god. If every weapon was taken from their hands and all the young men were gone, with clenched fists those who were left would smite and smite to the last. It is, fitting that they should feel this way, but I'm glad that our English boys can still laugh while they die.

And now I'm going out on the *boulevards* to get lunch.

28

Paris

January 30, 1918

Yesterday on my return to Paris I found all your letters awaiting me—a real big pile which took me over an hour to read. The latest was written on New Year's Day in the throes of coal shortage and intense cold. Really it seems absurd that you should be starved for warmth in America. Last week I was within eighteen kilometres of the front-line staying in a hotel as luxurious as the Astor, with plenty of heat and a hot bath at midnight in a private bathroom. All the appointments and comforts were perfect; booming through the night came the perpetual muttering of the guns. There were troops of all kinds marching up for an attack; the villages were packed, but there was no disorganisation.

Well, I've had a great trip this last time. I went to see refugee work—and saw it. There were barracks full of babies—the youngest only six days' old. There were very many children who have been recaptured from the Huns.

Tomorrow I start off for the borders of Switzerland to see the repatriated French civilians arrive. Then I go with the head of the Red Cross for a tour to see the reconstruction work in the devastated districts. When that is finished, I return to London to put my book together. I hope to get back to my battery about the end of March.

What a time I have had. A year ago it would have seemed impossible. I've motored, gone by speeders and trains to all kinds of quiet and ancient places which it would never have entered my head to visit in peace times. The American soldier is everywhere, striking a strange note of modernity and contrast. He sits on fences through the country-side, swinging his legs and smoking Bull Durham, when he isn't charging a swinging sack with a bayonet. He is the particular pal of all the French children.

I'm now due for a day of interviews and shall have to ring off. I rose at seven this morning so as to write this letter. At the moment I'm sitting in a deep armchair, with an electric lamp at my elbow. It's an awful war! In less than two months I'll be sitting in clothes that I haven't taken off for a fortnight—the mud will be my couch and the flash of the guns my reading lamp. It's funny, but up there in the discomfort I shall be ten times more happy.

29

Paris
February 13, 1918

I've not heard from you for two weeks—which is no fault of yours. There was a delay in getting passports—so I'm only just back from the devastated districts and get on board the train for London tonight. It's exactly six weeks today since I left England on this adventure.

I've done a good many things since last I wrote you. Did I tell you that among others I visited Miss Holt's work for the blind? I can think of nothing which does more to call out one's sympathy than to sit among those sightless eyes. I have talked about courage, but these men leave me appalled and silent. They are covered with decorations—the *Legion d'Honneur*, etc. They all have their stories. One, after he had been wounded and while there was still a chance of saving his sight, insisted on being taken to his general that he might give information about a German mine. When his mission was completed, his chance of ever seeing again was ended.

On the way back I saw Joffre walking. I now know why they call him Papa Joffre. He is huge, ungainly and white and kind. Somehow he made me think of a puppy—he had such an air of surprise. There was a premature touch of spring in the tree-tops. The grand old man of France was aware of—it he looked as though it were his first spring, so young in an ancient sort of way. He was stopping all the time to watch the sparrows flying and the shrubs growing misty with greenness. For all his braid and decorations he looked like an amiable boy of splendid size.

And then I went to Amiens. When I was in the line, it was always my dream to get there. Our senior officers used to play hooky in Amiens and come back with wonderful tales of sheeted beds and perpetual baths. I got there towards evening and was met by a British staff officer with a car. After dinner I escaped him and wandered through the crooked streets, encountering everywhere my dearly beloved British Tommy, straight out of the trenches for a few hours' respite.

As I passed estaminets I could hear concertinas being played and voices singing. It was London and heroism and homesickness all muddled up together that these voices sang. And they sang just one song. It is the first song I heard in France, when the war was very much younger. When the war is ended, I expect it will be the last. If the war goes on for another thirty years, our Tommies will be singing it—wheezing it out on concertinas and mouth-organs, in rain and sunshine, on the line of march, on leave or in their cramped billets. Invincible optimists that they are—so ordinary, so extraordinary, so good-humoured and mild! I peered in through the estaminets' windows of Amiens— there they sat with their equipment off, their elbows on the table and their small beer before them. And here's what they sang, as so many who are dead have sung before them:

Apres la guerre fini
Tons les soldats parti,
Mademoiselle 'ave a souvenir—
Apres la guerre fini.

After all my wandering along French and American fronts, I was back among my own people.

My final night in Amiens was equally typical. I went to the officers' club and found a sing-song in progress. There was a cavalry-major there who had been in the show at Cambrai. He was evidently a hunting-man, for he kept on getting off his hunting calls whenever things threatened to become dull. Most of the music was rag-time, which offended him very much. "Let's sing something English," he kept on saying. So we gave him *John Peel, Hearts of Oak, Drink to me only with thine Eyes*—and he went to bed happy.

I had a good fast car, so using Amiens as our base we struck into the Aisne, Oise and Somme, covering a good many kilometres a day. In these districts the Huns were masters a year ago—and now we are ploughing. The enemy withdrew from these districts last March. Nearly all the demolition is wilful and very little of it is due to shell-fire. In town after town scarcely a house is left standing—everything is gutted. The American Red Cross is trying to do something to alleviate this distress. It was in a ruined *chateau* I found the Smith College Unit and, much to my surprise, Miss W. from Newark, who had just received a letter from M. She was wanting to go to Amiens, so we put her in the car and took her back with us.

I'm longing to get to England to read all your letters and Papa's book and preface. I feel quite out of touch. Tomorrow I shall be in London.

I was in Paris when the Huns were overhead and saw one of them come down. The calmness of the people was amazing. There was no dashing for the Métro or other funk holes; only a contemptuous cheeriness. The French are great.

30

London
February 18, 1918

Today I have made a start on my book *Out to Win*, and miss you very much. It's quite a difficult thing, I find, to really concentrate on literary work in a strange environment. I wish I could take a magic powder and find myself back in my own little study, with my own little family, till the book is written.

Today I re-read Papa's book, which is very poignant and magnanimous and splendid.

Heaps of people I met in France were returning to America, and promised to telephone you to say they had seen me.

I stumbled across a most inspiring conversation which I overheard the other day, and which, if I had time, I would work into a story, entitled *His Bit*.

I was sitting in front of two women on a bus.

"Well," said one, "when they told me that Phil was married, you could 'ave knocked me darn wiv a feather."

It transpired that Phil was a C. 3 class man, no good for active service. He had met a girl, turned out into the streets by her parents because she was about to have a child by a soldier now

148

dead, whom she had not married. Phil, without asking her any questions, did his "bit"—led her off and married her right away because he was sorry for her.

"And she ain't a wicked girl," said one of the good ladies on the bus. "She didn't mean no harm. She was just soft-like to a Tommy on leave, I expect. It was 'ard lines on 'er. But that Phil—my goodness, he'll make 'er a good 'usband. Is the child born? I should just fink so. 'E's that proud, she might be 'is own darter. 'E carries 'er raund all over the plaice, Lord bless yer. And 'is wife's people, they can't make too much of 'im. No, 'e's not strong—a C. 3 man. I thought I told yer. She 'as ter work to 'elp 'im along. But between 'em—. There! I'm 'ate h'orf to Phil. They're a bloomin' pair of love-birds."

I like to think of Phil, don't you? I like to know that chaps like him are in the world. He couldn't fight the Germans; but he could play the man by a dead soldier.

That's a little bit of real life to help you along. Now I'm going to knock off and rest.

31

London
February 24, 1918

I'm not spending much time on letter-writing just at present. From morning till night, just as I did when I was writing *The Glory of the Trenches*, I shove away at my new book. I am most anxious to get it creditably finished and soon. The weather is getting quite ripping for the front and I'm keen to be back in time for the spring offensive.

You'll be pleased to know that, under my encouragement, your youngest son has broken out into literature. He did it while I was away in France. And the result is extraordinarily fine. He's managed to fling the spirit of his job on paper—it lives and gets you. When they are asked at the end of a patrol what they have been doing, they answer, "Pushing Water"—so that he's made that answer his title.

When I took the manuscript to W., he said:"But haven't you

another brother? What's he doing? Where's his manuscript? And what about your mother and sister in America, and your sister in Holland? Don't tell me that they're not all writing?"

At that moment I felt a deep sympathy for Solomon, who I'm sure must have been a publisher. Only a publisher would say so tiredly: "Of making many books there is no end."

On Tuesday another beastly birthday is due me—but I shan't say anything about it. I shall commence my new lease of life with a meat-card in my hand and no prospect of being really fully fed till I get back to France. For the first time England is feeling a genuine shortage. She isn't particularly annoyed at being rationed, but the worry you have over finding out how much you are allowed to eat and where and when causes people a good deal of trouble. My own impression is that there is plenty of food in England at present, but that we want to conserve it in order to be able to lend America our tonnage.

32

London
March 19, 1918

Below my window, as I write, I can hear the stirring of the Strand. Newsboys are calling the latest papers, motor-horns hoot and the million feet of London, each pair with their own separate story, chatter against the pavement. What a world! How do we ever get tired of living! Every day there are new faces, bringing new affections and adventure, new demands for tenderness and strength. These footsteps will go on. They will never grow quiet. A thousand years hence they will clatter along these pavements through the miracle of recreation. Why do we talk of death and old age? It is not true that we terminate. Even in this world the river in whose movement we have our part, still goes on—the river of opinions, of effort, of habitation.

The sound of us dies faint up the road to the listener who stands stationary; but the fact that at last he ceases to hear us does not mean that we have ceased to exist—only that we have gone farther. How arbitrary we are in our petty prejudices against immortality! God hears more distinctly the travellers to whom men have ceased to listen. Nothing to me is more certain than that we go on and on, drawing nearer to the source of our creation through the ages. Just as I came home to you after so many risks, such suffering, elation, bloodshed, so through the unthinkable adventure of time we journey home to our Maker. Going out of sight is sad, as are all partings. But I can bear to part now in a way that I could not before I saw the heavens open in the horror of war. I have ceased to be afraid of the unguessable, and better still I have lost my desire to guess. Not to stand still—to press onwards like soldiers—that is all that is required of us. I have heard men talk about world-sorrows, but if you trace them back, our sorrows are all for ourselves they are a personal equation. To develop one's personality in the remembering of others seems to me to be the only road to happiness. All this talk— why? Because of the foot-steps beneath my window!

The leave train has just arrived at Charing Cross from France. It steamed across the Thames with the men singing *The Land Where the Bluebells Grow*. There was laughter and longing in their singing.

33

Bath
March 24, 1918

Here I am with Mr. Lane, spending the weekend. It's a wonderful spring Sunday—no hint of war or anything but flowers and sunshine.

An hour ago I halted outside the newspaper office and read the latest telegrams of the great German offensive. It seemed like the autumn of 1914, reading of death and not being a part of it. They'll not take very long in letting me get back to my battery now. One's curiously egotistic—I feel, if only I were out there, that with my little bit of extra help everything would go well.

Yesterday we went to a fine old Jacobean house to tea—the kind of house that one has dreamt of possessing. There were high elms with rooks cawing and green lawns with immaculately gravelled paths. Inside there were broken landings and rooms with little stairs descending, and panelling, and pictures—everything for which one used to care. The late Belgian ambassador to England was there—a sad, courteous man. As we walked back with him to Bath along the canal, he remarked casually that all the art-treasures in his *chateau* outside of Brussels had been shipped to Germany.

We spent the afternoon seeing the king's pictures—mostly Gainsboroughs—which have been brought to Bath from the palace. From here we went to tea with an old lady who rode on her lonesome through Persia many years ago and consequently has gained a Lady Hester Stanhope reputation and, what is more important, a splendid selection of Eastern carpets and silver-work.

After that we walked home by way of the great crescent which forms the scene in *The School for Scandal*.

An odd day to. dodge in between experiences of European war! I have to pinch myself awake to remember what is happening at this moment in the front-line trenches. Probably within a few weeks I shall be there—and feeling very much more contented with myself than I do now.

34

London
March 31, 1918

Eric is with me. I am very glad to have him for my last days in England, and I do hope that Reggie may get here in time to see me. He's ordered south in two weeks' time, but I may be in France by then. I report at Canadian headquarters tomorrow, and will probably be sent straight down to camp, and from there to France within two weeks.

Have you seen General Currie's stirring message to the Canadians, saying that he expects them to die to a man if, by so doing, they can push the Huns back? This summer will see the biggest of all the battles. I'm wildly excited and longing to get back. There'll be some of the old glamour about this new fighting—it's all in the open. We've got away from trench warfare at last.

The beasts are all over the country which we fought for and have recaptured since 1916. They've destroyed for a second time all there construction work that I saw in the devastated areas. I'm wondering if all the girls got out in time. There were so many American girls there. Don't you dear people get down in the mouth when I'm again at the front. It's where I've wanted to be for a great many months ever since I recovered. To be able to go back now, when there's really something doing, is very fitting. I should have been wasting my time, perhaps, during the inactivity of the winter, if I'd been sitting in dugouts when I might have been writing *Out to Win*. But no man, whatever his capacities, is wasting his time in fighting at this hour of crisis. I've been made ashamed by the excuses I've heard put up for various quitters who have taken bomb-proof jobs. I'm in terror lest I should be confused with such.

Heaven knows, I'm no fonder of killing or of being killed than anyone else, but there are times when everything decent responds to the demand of duty. I shall absolutely be immensely happy to be a man again, taking my chances. I know that you will be glad for me. If you hadn't known for certain that I was going back, you'd have been making excuses for me in your hearts during these last five months. Papa's book would have been an anti-climax—he might still have been the father of a son in khaki, but not of a soldier. So smile and be proud. And whatever happens, go on being proud and smiling. Your job is to set an example. That's your contribution towards winning the war.

It's past midnight, and I go to camp tomorrow. I'll let you have a cable when I go to the front—so you needn't be nervous.

35

In Camp. England
April 4, 1918
I got down here last night and reported back this morning.

153

I found the general of my division had already applied for me, so I am going back to my old brigade at the beginning of this week on the Sunday, I think. Today is Wednesday, so I haven't lost much time in getting into action. Probably I shall go up to London tomorrow for a two days' leave and meet Eric. There's just a chance that Reggie may be with us as well, for I've sent him a telegram to say that I'm going to France.

And now, as you may imagine, I am at last happy and self-respecting. I'm going to be a part of the game again and not a pretence-soldier. What's more, I'm going to go straight into a real—battle the biggest of the war. It's really splendid and I feel childishly elated.

Well, I've had a run for my money if any man ever had. The good times in England, France and America will be worth re-membering when I'm again in the righting. I contrast in my mind my present mood with that of the first time when I went out—I was very much afraid then; now I'm extraordinarily hap-py. I've learnt to appreciate the privilege of being in the glory and the heroism. I'm more pleased than if I had won a decora-tion, that my colonel should have asked for my return at the first possible moment. It proves to me something which one often doubts—that I really am some good out there.

Keep your tails up, my dear ones, and don't get worried. This line is only to let you know the good news.

36

London
April 6, 1918

I'm the happiest person in London today at the thought of my return. This is quite unreasonable, when I sit down to cal-culate the certain discomfort and danger. I can't explain it, un-less it is that only by being at the front can I feel that I am living honourably. I've been self-contemptuous every minute that I've been out of the line. I began to doubt myself and to wonder whether all my protestations of wanting to get back, were not a camouflage for cowardice. I can prove to myself that they weren't now. "The Canadians will advance or die to a man" were the words that General Currie sent to his troops. Isn't it magnificent to be included in such a chivalrous adventure? I don't think you'll read about the Canadians retiring.

Whatever happens I've had a grand romance out of life—there's nothing of which to complain. I owe destiny no grudge. The world has been kind. I don't think I shall get killed; I never have thought that. But if I am, it will be as fine an ending to a full day's work as heart could desire.

I think I'm younger than I ever was. I no longer know satiety. The job in front of me fills all my soul and mind. I'm going to prove to myself and others that my books are not mere heroic sentiment. Going out a second time, despite the chances to hang back, will give a sincerity to what I've been trying to say to America. Heaps of people would think it brutal to want so much to go where men are being slaughtered—but it isn't the slaughtering that attracts, it's the winning of the ideal that calls me.

C. has command of my battery now. He's a fine chap. You remember how he left London before his leave was up, "because he wanted to be among men." That's the sort he is, and I admire him.

37

London
April 14, 1918

We're sitting together in the little flat at Battersea, and Reggie is with us. It's Sunday afternoon. Tomorrow morning early I set out for France. The little party wanted me to sleep here tonight so that they could get up about six a.m. and see me off. I wouldn't have that. So we're going to say goodbye comfortably tonight and the boys will sleep with me at a hotel just outside the station.

You can't guess how glad I am at the thought of going back. I was afraid I should never be a fighting man again. Now that I'm once more to be allowed to do my bit I feel extraordinarily grateful. I have the silly feeling that just one more man might make all the difference at such a crisis, and I'm jealous lest, when so many are being called upon for an exaggerated display of heroism, I should lose my chance. I know now why soldiers sing when they go out to war—they're so proud that they have been chosen for the sacrifice.

The boys came down to camp with me and lived near to the camp. I took an anti-gas defence course before rejoining in France. Friday night we came up to town and we've had a very jolly time.

Well, dears, we've lived a happy crowded life since I was wounded, and we've each one of us learnt more about the glory of this undertaking.

38

France
April 21, 1918

I've been back at the front six days. This is the first opportunity I have had to write. I left England last Monday, having spent Saturday and Sunday in London with the boys. Major H. came up to give me a send-off and we had a very gay time. Saturday evening, after dinner and a theatre, we returned to Battersea and all found beds in one or other of the flats. On Sunday evening we slept at a hotel next to the station so that I might be sure of catching the early morning train. We managed to get a room with three beds in it, and so kept all together as in the old days. By 5 a.m. we were up and stirring. P. and L. walked in on us as we were having breakfast, and S. met us on the platform. They all seemed quite assured that they would never, never see me again—which makes me smile.

I suppose they all had visions of gray waves of Germans deluging our infantry by force of numbers, while the gunners were left far in front, trying to stem the tide. That is what we all hope for. It's the kind of chance we dream about; but it hasn't happened yet.

Monday afternoon I was in France and slept at the base that

night. Early Tuesday morning I was on the move again, passing Red Cross trains packed with wounded and trucks crammed with ordnance. I couldn't help comparing this return to the Front with my first trip up. We had a good time playing cards and recalling the old fights—we were like schoolboys coming back for the holidays. There wasn't one of us who wasn't wildly excited at the thought of being a part of the game again. This was rather strange, if you come to consider it, for each of us had been wounded at least once and knew the worst of what war could do to us—yet fear was the emotion most remote from us. We were simply and sheerly glad to be going into the thick of it; our great fear had been that our fighting days were ended.

By 2 p.m. we were dumped out at a town through which I used to ride last summer. Here we had to report to the provost marshal for further transport orders. He told me that I should have to go to the corps reinforcement camp. I didn't intend to do that, so waited till he was engaged on the phone and then made my escape. Taking the baggage I could carry, I beat my way back to my old battery on foot and in lorries. I was just coming into the wagon-lines when I met Major C., who now commands us.

I think he had been lonely for some of the old faces; he went wild with delight. I had a magnificent welcome back. On the spur of the moment he made me a present of his own charger and took me up to the guns with him, where we arrived in time for a very late tea, within thirty-six hours of my leaving England.

The day after that I went forward to do my 24-hour spell at the observing station. When I saw my first Hun after so long an absence, I felt more like hugging him than trying to kill him. Of course I had to do the latter, and had a very nice little strafe. I wrote you a fine long letter up there and somehow lost it. So this is my second attempt.

Don't get nervous about me. Everything is quite all right with us and I'm having a real holiday after my feverish literary spasms. But a lot of familiar faces are absent.

39

France
April 22, 1918

You would hardly believe our peaceful state of mind unless you could drop in on us for an hour. You, in America, are evidently very worked up about us, and picture us as in desperate conditions. Don't worry, we've got our tails up and are happy as sand-boys. There's nothing of the grimly set faces about our attitude such as you imagine. We're too confident to be grim; war is actually, from our point of view, a gigantic lark. It must sound silly to you, I know, but I love to hear the screaming of the shells in the darkness and the baying of the guns. It's like a pack of wolves being chased through the night by bloodhounds.

I hadn't been back two days before they got the rumour at the wagon-lines that I was wounded—a little previous, I thought it. I call that wishing a blighty on me.

I've just come back from a trip across one of our old battlefields. We're in the Hun support-trenches, behind us is his front-line, then No Man's Land with its craters and graves, and behind that the front-line from which we jumped off. You can trace everything plainly and follow the entire attack by the broken wire and blown-in dugouts. We're still filled with amused contempt for the Hun on our part of the front.

We were discussing chaplains the other day—the way some of them have failed us in this war. One of the officers told a story of Grannie M., one of our first division majors. A chaplain, who never went further than the wagon-lines, was always saying how much he'd like to see the front. Grannie called his bluff and took him for a trip into one of the warmest spots. The chaplain kept dodging and crouching every time a shell fell within a hundred yards. Each time Grannie, standing quietly silent, waited for him to get up and renew the journey. At last the chaplain flopped into a shell-hole and refused to come out. Grannie, who is a big man and well over six foot, grinned down at him despisingly.

"Priest," he said, "if I thought I had half the pull with Christ that you say you have, not all the shells in France would make me lie as flat as that."

Later another chaplain came to that brigade. No one would give him house-room. He went off and slept where he could; he never came near the officers, but he haunted the men at the forward guns. When the brigade moved out to another sector, he procured an old skate of a horse and trailed along at the rear of the line of march like a hungry dog. The new front proved to be a warm one; there were many casualties, but the chaplain was always on his job, especially when the shells were falling.

From somewhere he got the money to start a canteen for the men, which he ran himself. When no one else had cigarettes, he could supply them. At last even the officers had to come to him. He finished up by being the most popular chaplain the brigade had ever had, honoured by everyone from the colonel down. There are your two types of army chaplains: the one who plays the game; the other who issues season tickets to heaven, but is afraid of travelling on them himself.

40

France
April 26, 1918

It is now over a week since I have been back with my battery and it seems as though all that trip along the American line and the rush back to New York had never happened. I'm sitting in a little "house" in a deep chalk trench. The house is made of half-circles of corrugated iron; there's an anti-gas blanket hanging at one end and at the other a window made of oiled calico. Up one corner are the maps, scales and office papers; pinned on boards is a four-foot map of the entire English front. My sleeping bag is stretched on an old French spring-mattress, which was brought here sometime ago by the Huns. From the walls hang a higgle-ty-pigglety of trench coats, breeches, tunics. This is the place in which we work out our ranges, play cards, have our meals and rest when we're back from doing forward work.

You can walk for miles where we are without ever being seen, if you follow the various systems of Hun and British trenches, for we're plumb in the heart of an old battlefield. The only landmarks left to guide one are the craters as big as churches records of mines that have been sprung and little rows of lonely graves. At night when the moon is up, this country creates the curious ghostly illusion of being an endless alkali desert, beaten into billows by the wind. The shells go shrieking over it and wreaths of mist wander here and there like phantoms. Destruction can create a terrible pretence and caricature of beauty. I wish you might visit such a place just once so as to get an idea of where our lives are spent.

Your letters *apropos* of the latest German offensive bring home to me very vividly the emotional terror which war excites in the minds of civilians. You picture us as standing with our backs to the wall, desperately pushing death from off our breasts with naked hands. The truth is so immensely different. We're having a thoroughly bang-up time, and we're as amused by the Hun as ever. He may force us to fall back; but while we fall back we laugh at him. That is the attitude of every British soldier that I've met. We're as happy and unconcerned as children.

There's one chap here who's typical of this spirit of treating war as an immensely sporting event. He's the raiding officer of a certain battalion, and is known as "Battling Brown"—though Brown is not his real name. He has a little company of his own, consisting of seventy men. He's been in over a hundred raids on the Hun Front-line and has only had two of his men killed in a year.

A short while ago he went across with his raiders and captured three Germans; on the return journey across No Man's Land something happened, and he lined up his prisoners and shot them. He led his men safely back to our lines and then set out again alone on a private excursion into the Boche territory. By dawn he once more returned, bringing back four prisoners single-handed. You might picture such a man as a kind of Hercules, but he isn't. He's thin, and tall, and fair, and high-strung. His age, I should guess, is about twenty-two.

Far away in the distance I can hear the pipers playing. It always makes me think of Loch Lomond and when we were little tads. How green and quiet and cool those days seem now—the long rides across the moors and down the glens, the bathing in little mountain streams, the walks in the sad twilights. There are so many happy memories I have to thank you for. You were very wise and generous in the way you planned my childhood. I'm less than a fortnight back at the front, but I'm already falling into the old habit of happy retrospect.

We don't live here really. Our souls are in France only for brief and glorious and intense intervals—during the moments of attack and repulse. The rest of the time we're away in the green valleys of remembered places, watching the ghosts who are the shadows of what we were.

My groom is a boy named Gilpin. The name has proved his downfall. He galloped my horse on the hard road the other day, which is forbidden. A colonel caught him going full tilt, stopped him and took his name. When the severities seemed ended this innocent young party asked the colonel to hold his horse while he mounted—so now he's up on an extra charge of insolence. Army discipline is in many ways silly and old-maidish. Here's a chap who's faithful, well-conducted and honest. He's likely to get a heavier punishment for asking a superior officer to hold his horse than if he'd been drunk and uproarious.

41

France
April 28, 1918

It's funny to recall all the different graveyards among the shell-holes that I've learnt to call home. Once life was so definitely focussed—much too definitely for my patience. It seemed as though I was rooted and planted for all eternity. It never seemed to me then that I should ever find the sacrificial opportunity or be stirred to any prophetic exaltations. It's wonderful the way the angel of Death, as discovered in war, can give one visions of limit-less nobilities, each one of which is attainable and accessible.

I'm by myself at the battery. It's late afternoon, and a thunderstorm is brewing. The room is dark (I mean the dugout); I feel as though it were November instead of April. What a queer life this is. In one way I have not had so much idleness since I was in hospital—then comes a burst of physical strenuosity out of all proportion to one's strength. Things happen by fits and starts; you never know what is going to happen next.

It's intensely still. The stillness is made more noticeable by the booming of an occasional gun.

The whole hope and talk of our chaps is the Americans-what they're going to do, when they're going to start doing it, and what kind of a morale they will have. I hear the wildest rumours of the numbers they have in France—rumours which I know to be untrue since my tour along the American lines. You will have read the manuscript of *Out to Win* long before this letter reaches you. I wonder what you all think of it and whether you like it. It was written in a breathless, racing sort of fashion. I sat at it from morning till last thing at night. All my desire was to do my duty as regards the Americans and then to get out here before the big show started. I managed things just in time. I don't remember much of what I wrote—only a picture of Domrèmy and another of Evian and Nancy. I hope it was as good as you expected.

There are things one lives through and sees now which seem ordinary, but which to future ages will figure as stupendous. If one can record them now in just that spirit of ordinariness which constitutes their real wonder, they will together give an accurate portrait of Armageddon. My nine months out of the line began to give me a little perspective—I began to see the awful marvellousness of some of the scenes that I had lived through. Now, like the mist which I see hanging above the Hun front-line, a curtain of normality is blotting out the sharp abnormal edges of my landscape.

This war, at the distance which removes you from it, must seem a filthy and brutal kind of game. It is all of that. But it's more than that. The game was not of our inventing—it was thrust on us. We are not responsible for the game; but we are responsible for the spirit in which we play it. The fine, clear, visionary attitude of our chaps redeems for us the horror and *pathos* of the undertaking.

It will be towards the end of May when this arrives and you'll be off to the lakes and the mountains. I wonder where. I suppose we'll still be plugging along, sending death over into Fritzie's lines and receiving it back.

42

France
May 2, 1918

Here I am up forward again on my shift. I'm sitting in a hole sunk beneath the level of the ground, with a slit that just peeps out across the dandelions to the Hun front-line. From here I can catch any movement in the enemy back-country without being seen myself. Below my O.P. there is a deep dugout to which I can retire in the event of enemy shelling; if one exit gets blown in, there's a second from which I can make good my escape.

On each fresh trip to this place I find a new gem of literature left behind by one or other of the telephonists. Last time it was a priceless kitchen masterpiece by Charles Garvice, entitled *The Triumphant Lover*; this time it's an exceedingly purple effort by Victoria Cross, entitled *Five Nights*. So you see I do not allow my interest in matters intellectual to rust.

There are many things of interest that I should like to tell you, but the consciousness that the censor is forever at my elbow prevents. Did I ever tell you the story of the censor, whom I met on the train from Boulogne, when I was returning to the line in January, 1917. If I happened to tell it to you, the gentleman who uninvited shares all my letters with you hasn't heard it, and I'm sure his curiosity must be pricked by this time—so here goes.

It was after that splendid leave in London, which you came over from America to share with me. The train from Boulogne to the front was the usual draughty affair, half the windows out, no heating system, no means of getting anything to eat for good-ness knows how many hours. I picked out the least disreputable carriage and found that a gunner colonel was snuggled up in one corner and a pile of rugs, pillows, hot-water bottles, eatables, etc., in another.

Just as the train was starting the owner of all these effeminate luxuries hopped in and commenced to make himself comfortable. He was nearer fifty than forty. His nose was inflamed and heavily veined, either from drink, dyspepsia or both. His rank was that of a lieutenant. His social grade that of a post-office assistant, I should fancy. His uniform fitted abominably and his appearance was as unsoldierly as can well be imagined. He looked like a loose-living spider.

We hadn't been moving very long, when he started to unwrap his packages and to gorge himself. He eat steadily like one whose life depended on it. The colonel and I had forgotten to bring anything, so we had the joy of watching.

In our chilly misery we became human and began to talk. The conversation became reminiscent of the numerous offensives. The sloppy lieutenant with the drooping walrus moustaches who sat opposite to us, persistently laid claim to a more thorough knowledge of attacks that we had been in than we did ourselves.

He puzzled us; we couldn't picture him as a combatant. Quite haphazard one of us—I think it was the colonel—commenced to damn censors as chaps who sat safely behind the lines and spied on fighting-men's private affairs.

The lieutenant became very hot in the censors' defence. He tried to prove the necessity for them by quoting the case of a lieutenant named N., who had sent back captured aeroplane photos to his friends. I happened to know N. and that he was going to be tried by court-martial for his indiscretion, so grew loud in proclaiming my contempt for the fellow safely behind the lines who had caught him. We were particularly annoyed because N. was a plucky soldier.

Our friend in the corner took my remarks extremely personally. To show his resentment of me, he pointedly offered the colonel some of his fodder. At last he said very haughtily, "It may interest you to know that I am the censor and am at present going up the line to give evidence against Lieutenant N. at his trial."

Just at that moment the train stopped at a station. He blinked through the window with his short-sighted eyes, trying to read the name. "This is M., I think," he said; "if it is, we stop here ten minutes and get time to stretch our legs."

I looked out of the window helpfully. "It is M.," I told him. It wasn't. He got out and commenced to walk up the platform. Almost immediately the train started to pull out. He made a wild crab-wise dash for the carriage-door, but the colonel and I were hanging to it on the inside. When we were safely on our journey, we shared up his pillows, rugs, hot-water bottles and eatables between us, and had a comparatively pleasant journey. For once we thanked God for the censor.

It's tea-time at home. You've probably come in from a walk and are smoking a cigar at the family oak-table. I wish I could pop in on you.

O, our latest excitement! We received our new gramophone last night with about thirty of the latest records!

You'll be glad to know that I now have my old batman back. He's the man who took me out when I was wounded and was so tender to me on the way to the hospital. That memory of his tenderness is rather embarrassing, for I can't bring myself to strafe him the way I ought to. I can always see the fellow's concern when he thought that I was done for.

Now that he's got me back he acts as though I were still a very weak and indiscreet person who had to be coaxed and managed. I have the feeling in his presence of being perpetually in pyjamas and in bed. He has the advantage of me, to put it in a nutshell.

43

May 3, 1918

It's early morning. I'm still sitting in the little dugout with the slit that looks towards the Hun front-line.

Everything but the immediate foreground is blanketed in heavy mist at present. I can hear bombing going on somewhere but I can also hear a lark singing near to the sun, high overhead. The clumps of dandelions are still sleeping. They haven't opened—they're green instead of yellow. The grass sparkles with little drops of dew, more beautiful than the most costly diamonds.

With the first of the dawn I read a story by Tolstoi; since then I've been sitting thinking—thinking of you and of the sleeping house in Newark, which will soon be disturbed by Papa's bathwater running, if he still rises early; and thinking how strange it is that I should be here in the greatest war in history. We planned to do such different things with our lives. My first dream was to become extremely wise. At Oxford there seemed no limit to the amount of knowledge I could acquire; it seemed only a matter of patience and perseverance.

Then that dream went, and I wanted to save the world. I'm afraid one has to be a little aristocratic towards the world before he can conceive of himself as capable of saving it or of the world as requiring saving.

The aristocratic touch grew on me and I decided to do my saving not by touching people, but by writing poetry for the few who would understand. It wasn't half such good poetry as I thought it was at the time and it never could have remade anything.

Disappointed in that and because I had now committed myself to a literary way of life, I took to writing novels, which nobody wanted to publish, read or buy. Then, because I had to live somehow, I entered into the commercial end of publishing.

There was always the shadow of a dream which I pursued even then in my spare hours; it was the dream that saved me and led me on to write *The Garden Without Walls*. But the shadow was growing fainter when this war commenced. And here I am, human at last, all touch of false aristocracy gone, peeping out across the grass wet with the dew of May, beneath which lie the common clay heroes who have died for democracy. How noiselessly these men gave up their lives and with how little consciousness of self-appreciation.

They rather put us to shame we privileged dawdlers in our haunted minds. They recognised the one straight thing to do when the opportunity presented itself; they did it swiftly and unreasoningly with their might.

They didn't write about what they did; for them the doing was sufficient. I think I shall always be a humble man after such companionship, if I survive. I see life in courageous *vistas* of actions now; formerly I was like Hamlet—I thought myself into a green sickness. Marriage and children, a home and family love are the best that anyone can extract from life. There have been years when I didn't like my kind.

Out of the many things that have come to me in the past six months I am particularly glad of little Tinker's friendship—P.'s baby. She's not two yet, but we were real pals. She would never go to sleep until I had kissed her in her cot "Goodnight."

First thing in the morning she would be beside my bed, tugging at the clothes and ordering me to "Det up." Since I've been gone they've had to ring the bell and pretend that I'm just entering the hall, so that they may make her go to sleep contented.

When they ask her, "Where's Con?" she reaches up to the window and points. "Dorn walk in park," she says. They talk about the love of a woman keeping a man straight, but I don't think it's to be compared with the love of a little child. You can't lie to them.

The sharp *rat-a-tat* of the machine-guns has started; but the mist is too thick for me to see what is happening . It's nothing; it's died down.

In an hour I shall be relieved, and shall return to the guns and post this letter. It will reach you when? Sometime in June, I expect, when the summer is really come and you're wearing your cool dresses. I can see you going out in the early morning to do your shopping.

44

France
May 7, 1918

I am sitting in my bed—my sleeping-sack I mean—which is spread out on the red-tiled floor of a funny little cottage. There isn't much of the floor left, as four of the other officers are sharing the room with me. Coming in through the window is the smell of sweet-myrtle, old-fashioned and quiet; from far away drifts in the continual pounding of the guns and, strangely muddled up with the gunfire, the multitudinous croaking of frogs. I'm having an extraordinary May month of it in lovely country, marching through the showers, getting drenched and drying when the sun deigns to make an appearance. After being off a horse for so long, I'm in the saddle for many hours every day.

I am glad that you all feel the way you do about my returning to the front. I was sure you wouldn't want me to be out of these great happenings. My fear, when I was in England this spring, was the same as I had when I first joined—that fighting would all be ended before I got into the line. No fear of that; I think we're in for another two years of it. There's hot work ahead-the hottest of the entire war. Oddly enough my spirits rise as the struggle promises to grow fiercer. I don't know why, unless it is that as the action quickens one has a chance of giving more. There's nothing sad about being wounded or dying for one's country. In this war one does so much more than that—he dies for the whole of humanity.

Outside my window a stretch of hedges runs down to a little brook. Ducks, geese, cocks and hens make farmyard noises from dawn till last thing at night. Above all the peace and quiet, the distant guns keep up their incessant murmur. What a variety of places are likely to shelter me before the summer is ended-woods, ditches, open fields, trenches. It's all in the game and is romance of a sort. I'm sunburnt and hard. I feel tremendously alive.

Once again all the striving and ambition of literary success has vanished. I'm only a subaltern—and far prouder to be that than a writer. I'm estimated by none but my soldiering qualities and power to show guts. We were lawyers, engineers, business-men—now we're soldiers and enquire nothing of each other's past.

A thrush has started singing; he's in the willows that stand by the brook-side. The planes go purring overhead, but he doesn't care. He goes on singing towards the evening sun as though his heart knew nothing but joy. He will be here singing long after we have passed upon our way.

Don't get worrying about my safety. You're sure to be feeling nervous at the wrong times, when I'm perfectly safe. Just feel glad that I'm allowed to be here, and don't look ahead.

45

France
May 14, 1918

I'm afraid you'll be feeling that I've neglected you. Whenever I miss a mail I have the reproachful picture of the disappointed faces of you three at the early morning breakfast—so it isn't wil-ful neglect. I've had no time, for reasons which I can't explain. In this way of life one has to snatch the odd moments for those he loves best and to break off when the sterner obligations intrude themselves.

I'm in a beautiful part of the country at present—it must be beautiful, for it is providing us with three ducks for dinner tonight. I doubt whether you could get three all at once in Ne-wark. Moreover we can get all the fresh cream and butter that we like. Of course this won't last. Any morning we may wake up to find ourselves back on iron rations—bully-beef and hard tack. But while it lasts we make the most of it. The most ripping attraction to me is something that you'll scarcely credit. The willow-groves are full of nightingales.

As you go back to your billets after midnight and the guns make lightning through the grill-work of the trees, you see the little brown fellows with their throats quivering, pouring out their song of love and spring. When you've crept into your sleeping-sack, you lie awake listening thinking of another world where love and life were once so certain.

46

France
May 18, 1918

This is the third day that I have planned to write you. Perhaps I may be able to do so this time.

I have just been reading a letter from a nurse out in Palestine describing the little wooden crosses above fallen British soldiers which now star the Mount of Olives. The poetry of the ordinary crops out everywhere today; we are living on higher levels than we realise. For hundreds of years the future generations will weave legends round us, making us appear Titanic spirit-people, just as we have clothed with almost unearthly splendour the Crusaders of the Dark Ages.

This is a pleasant May evening. The fields are golden with buttercups. Above the singing of the birds I can hear a low droning as of bees among flowers; but the droning is of homing aeroplanes. This is the kind of weather and country in which it would not be unbeautiful to die.

When I went down this morning to the barn in which my section is stationed, I found "Notice" printed on the door, on either side a British and American flag, and underneath a luridly illustrated Sunday magazine selection of extracts from *The Glory of The Trenches*. A small world, isn't it?

I have been reading a book lately that would interest you; it's by Ford Madox Hueffer and is called *On Heaven*. It consists of a number of poems written while on active service. He's managed to put down in a rough and tumble of words a good many of our hungers and adorations. I hadn't realized before I read him how very much of the conversation of our soldiers is an exchange of confidences about the women they love or have loved. I believe every man at the front has a hope of the girl he will be true to some day and a fear lest—

One of Hueffer's poems on the subject is very beautiful. It

starts this way:

In Chepstow stands a castle;
My love and I went there;
The foxgloves on the wall all heard
Her footsteps on the stair.
The sun was high in heaven
And the perfume in the air
Came from purple cat's valerian—
But her footsteps on the stair
Made a sound like silver music
Thro' the perfume in the air.

The last verse sums up the dread of many a fighting-man that all his dreams are only dreams and that a return to reality may disappoint him:

And another soldier fellow
Shall come courting of my dear.
And it's I shall not be with her
With my lips beside her ear.
For it's he shall walk beside her
In the perfume of the air
To the silver silver music
Of her footstep on the stair

All the world's idealists are in the trenches by now. What a shining cloud of imaginings must rise up to the Soul which lies behind the world. God must be amazed to find that horror can make His obstinate creations so simple and childlike. Here are millions of us who once thought only of our social and individual bellies, now thinking only of the unborn children and the things of the spirit. All the fond and dear accepted affections have become a kind of heaven that lies in the past, instead of the future. If we die, we don't want any heaven that isn't a re-living of the old happy memories.

I find that Hueffer expresses a feeling that many of us have secretly, but which I have never heard any man acknowledge-the feeling that all the remainder of his days he will have to be explaining if he comes to the end of the war alive almost the feeling that he will have lost his great chance of nobility by not dying. Hueffer's poem is called *One Day's List*; it's a list of three officers and 270 other ranks of his regiment who were killed in action. It commences,

My dears,
The rain drips down on Rouen Town,
The leaves drip down
And so the mud
Turns orange brown.

And it has for its refrain,

But you—at least—are out of it.

It goes on to tell of the officers who fell and repeats the reflection which we all have when we gaze on the dead at the end of an attack and know that we ourselves have escaped,

One wonders why you died.

And then,

We never talked of glory,
And each thought a lot of one girl,
And waited most days for hours in the rain
Till she came:
But we never talked of Fame—

And lastly, addressing the dead,

But we who remain shall grow old,
We shall know the cold
Of cheerless
Winter and the rain of Autumn and the sting
Of poverty, of love despised and of disgraces.
And mirrors showing stained and ageing faces,
And the long ranges of comfortless years
And the long gamut of human fears—

But, for you, it shall be forever Spring,
And only you shall be forever fearless,
And only you have white, straight, tireless limbs,
And only you, where the water-lily swims
Shall walk along the pathways, thro' the willows
Of your west.
You who went west,
And only you on silvery twilight pillows
Shall take your rest
In the soft sweet glooms,
Of twilight rooms—

There's the whole of our one and only cowardice in a nut-shell—that we, who have posed as conquerors for a while, will, if we survive, return to the normal things of life to find our spirits unexalted and the commonplace still commonplace.

Out here, where there are corpses in the thistles and *"the gas-shells burst like snow"* we can talk of *"the silver, silver music of her footsteps on the stair,"* but we're mortally afraid that in less exult-ant moments, when the heart is not so starved for affection, we shall discover that the "silver music" is only the irritating sound of squeaky shoes.

I can't hear from you again for at least six days—a long time to wait! I can't be bothered now-a-days to let the mail-clerk sort out the letters: I grab the bag and go through it myself.

There may be an interval between this letter and those that follow. If there is, don't worry yourselves. It is not possible to find the time or place to write under all circumstances.

47

France
June 1, 1918

I can't remember when last I wrote you. It isn't always easy to get the time. Recently I've spent a good many hours in the saddle and have been up early in the morning; when work is done the fresh air leaves one too tired for anything but sleep. But you mustn't worry about me. I'm stronger than I've been for months and tanned to the colour of an Indian.

I have recently met the doctor who did so much to pull me through when I was wounded last June at the casualty clearing station. He's still the same tall, thin, silent man, with the kindest and sternest of faces. His brother, he tells me, is in America on the British Mission and had informed him of America's immense preparations. Like all the men out here, I found him keenly eager to see the U.S.A. proportionately represented in the front-line. We are holding, and counting on the States to turn the tide dramatically in our favour. Our chaps are quite calm and confident of success—out here there's none of the strain and nervousness which is felt by civilians. Our chaps are as philosophical and cheery as ever.

"Good old Fritz," they say "so he's taken another fifteen miles! Well, it'll be our turn next." Through defeat and success we carry on quite normally and unperturbed, confident of ultimate victory. The general opinion is that the Hun by his advances is only causing himself a lot of unnecessary trouble, as he'll have a longer distance to run back to Germany.

Here's the first of June and midsummer approaching when so many pleasant things used to happen—flights to the country, the purchasing of bathing-suits, fishing-nets, maps—the planning of such quantities of family adventures. It would be happy to think that some of these old pleasures might return one day. The longer the war goes on the more impossible it is to conjure up the picture of civilian ways of life or to see oneself as again in the picture. Everything grows blurred except the present, with the early risings, routine, orders, marches and attacks. To be given our freedom would leave us dazed.

This will probably reach you after you have left New York and settled down for the holidays in some quiet country place. There's only one spot which seems permanent in our family life—the little gray shack among the orchards in the Rockies. My thoughts fly to it very often these hot summer days. I see the lake like a blue mirror, reflecting the mountains and the clouds. I hear the throbbing of the launch. Bruce is barking on the wharf. Figures are moving about the boat-house. We climb the hill together where the brook sings through the flowers and the evening meal awaits us. And afterwards those long sleepy evenings when the dusk comes down and the flowers shine more vaguely, and we talk so endlessly, planning books, retraversing the past, mapping out a road to so many future El Dorados. I can remember these former happinesses without self-torture or regret. The present is so splendid that it outshines all former beauties. I go forward happily, believing that any bend of the future may bring the old kindnesses into view again.

The old haunting dream of Blighty is growing up in me once again—the Blighty we speak of, think of, worship and imagine every hour of the day. It's worth being wounded if only to wake up the first morning in the long white English ward, with the gold-green sunlight dripping in from the leaves through the open windows. These are the exquisite moments of peace and rest which come to one in the midst of warfare. Of such moments within the last year I have had my share; they are happy to remember.

And the war goes on and on. I was so afraid that it would be ended before ever I got back. The fear was needless. I shall be out here at least another year before peace is declared. There are times when I think that the Americans are not so far wrong in their guess when they give themselves "four years to do this job." The Hun may be desperate; his very energy may be a proof of his exhaustion. But his death struggle is too vigorously successful to promise any very rapid end.

Our hope is in America, with her high courage, her sacrifice and her millions of men. If she had not joined us, we would still stand here chaffingly and be battered till not one of us was left. The last one would die with the smile of victory on his mouth. Whatever happens, they'll never catch any British fighting-man owning that his tail is down. But the thought of the American millions gives us confidence that, though we are wiped out, we shall not have lost. Like runners in a relay race, though we are spent, the pace we have set will enable those who come after us to win in the last lap.

But don't worry about me. I'm having splendid run for my money and am far more happy than I deserve.

48

France
June 1, 1918

As per usual when I write to you, I have my nose up against a solitary candle, am hedged in by shadows and have the stump of a cigarette in my mouth. For days I have been waiting for letters from home, but none have arrived as yet. Either the ship has gone down or some other calamity has happened. I now promise myself that tomorrow there will be a huge package of belated mail for me.

We're travelling very light at present. The first thing I did on my return was to cut down my kit to the barest necessities and send all the balance back to England. It's better to have it safe in London, if out of immediate reach, than to have to abandon it in a ditch or shell-hole. While the summer lasts there are a great number of things that one can do without.

What an unsportsmanly crowd the Germans are! I think more than anything else it will be their lack of fair play that we shall hold against them when war is ended. Yesterday at the Pope's request we were foolish enough to refrain from bombing Cologne, so the Hun took the opportunity to both bomb and shell the Catholics of Paris. It makes one itch to grab a bayonet and go over the top to do him as much damage as opportunity will allow. The Hun is educating us out of our good-humoured contempt into a very deep-seated hatred of him.

The other day I was in a forward town recently evacuated by its population. You walked through silent, torn streets, the windows all broken by shells, the doors sagging from their hinges and open. You peered across the thresholds into the houses. In many cases meals were still on the tables, partly eaten and hastily left.

A stray cat scurried out into the yard; nothing else stirred.

Over the entire death-like silence the summer sun shone down and far away a cuckoo was calling. One gets accustomed to the outward symbols of such tragedies—the broken homes, abandoned security and foregone happiness. The people themselves get used to it. Today I met a farm-wagon piled high with the household gods, while a peasant woman walked beside with her best hat carried in a paper-bag in her hand. That was very typical—in all the ruin that had befallen a home to still cling to the best hat.

I'm very happy and well, living almost entirely in the open and in the saddle a good part of the day. The part of France I have lived in since my return is by far the cleanest and most beautiful that I have seen on active service. The weather has been golden and glorious. There is none of that fear in our hearts that you must experience for us. We're as certain of victory as we were during the days of the big Vimy advance.

The army is a nursery organisation, full of annoying pomposities and amusing class distinctions. Just at present we're being pestered with continual inspections, when each battery tries to invent some new trick for making itself look smarter. Soldiers, on such occasions, are like a lot of old women at a spring cleaning. The men much prefer killing Boches to being inspected. Burnishing steel, chasing all over the country to buy Brasso, spending fortunes on polish for the harness all seem such a fruitless waste of time when the Huns are hammering our line. But of course cleanliness has a moral effect on men who have been long under shell-fire.

This is a discursive sort of letter, and doesn't contain much real news. It's just for remembrance.

49

France
June 4, 1918

I've just left the gramophone shrilly declaring that "*When he fancies he is past love, it is then he meets his last love and he loves her as he never loved before.*" London comes with us to the front.

We hum the tunes of Piccadilly and Leicester Square, and we scheme such splendid times for our return. Leave has opened up again, but by a careful calculation I have discovered that it will take twenty-one years, four months and three days till my turn comes round at the present rate of allotments.

Some New York papers have just arrived and an exceedingly ancient cake, but no letters. In the midst of a great offensive it is wonderful that anything gets to us at all. We're as far away from you both in reality and imagination as though we lived in a different world. Our standards of conduct, normality, right living are not your standards—our hopes and fears are all different. Again, as when I first came to the front, everything civilian seems a tale I have read about.

I cannot believe that that person who was in New York last October was really myself. I rather wonder at him and at his capacity for writing about the commonplace events of the present life.

Now I couldn't write a line about the war if my life depended on it. I see nothing in perspective except the endless path of duty which leads on ahead as each day introduces itself. To what goal that path leads I sometimes try to guess—to something wonderful and unforeseen I have no doubt.

I judge from what I read that the entire world which is not at the front is anxious and depressed. We're just the same as ever cheery and waiting whatever may befall with a stoicism born of confidence. Our belief in ourselves, our cause and our ability to win, never wavers.

How extraordinarily normal we are you could hardly imagine. The moment our men get out of the trenches they begin to play baseball, football, cricket, etc. There's a big lake near to where we are with high red cliffs around it. Here every evening you can see the poised white figures of soldier men. Last Sunday we held aquatic sports there and had a fine display of swimming. It's wonderful to see the chaps so happy when you remember that nine-tenths of their companions of this time last year are either wounded or dead. As you may guess, we never in our

178

conversation call attention to this fact, though there can be few, if any, who forget.

There are children where we are at present. It's amusing to see them making friends with our boys. They slip their little paws into the big brown hands and toddle along quite proudly. I don't see how anyone could help loving our men—they're so simple. Their faults, when you know the hearts which they hide, become endearing. I think, especially when I see them with the French kiddies, "*Of such are the Kingdom of Heaven.*"

Please thank the donor of the cake which arrived today. We're eating it don't tell her it was dry.

50

France
June 7, 1918

Here's a glorious summer evening—the end of a perfect day during which I have done my share in capturing two German spies, who now repose unrestfully in our guard-room.

This morning, when I was leading a hundred mounted men along a road, a terrible thing happened. The road was narrow and on one side of it motor-lorries were standing; on the other side was a little unfenced river.

Suddenly and without warning, tearing down the hill ahead of us, came the enemy. The enemy consisted of a pair of mules harnessed to a heavy iron-roller. The roller caught my lead-driver and threw him and his two horses to the ground; then it charged on into the mass behind us. Miraculously no bones were broken; we all have nine lives.

Those mokes have put us up to a new trick for dispersing enemy cavalry which ought to be effective. Believe me, two mad mules, going thirty miles an hour with an iron-roller behind them, are utterly demoralising. It is impossible for any cavalry in the world to withstand them.

You don't know, can't guess, how letters from home buck me up and keep the lamp of my ideals still burning. There are moments when the mere mechanical side of warfare fills one's mind with an infinite depression. One sees men doing splendid acts, day in, day out, like automatons animated by the spring of duty. One almost forgets that there is any human element of choice in the matter or a difference between fighting and fighting well. When your pages come, I remember—remember that just such affections and human ties bind the hearts of all who are out here to life. I begin to see my chaps as personalities again and not as only soldiers.

Outside the chaps are singing *O my, I don't want to die; I want to go home*. Now they've changed to *Take me Over to Blighty*.

51

France
June 8, 1918

Last night I saw the old lady who nursed me up so that I was fit to come and meet you in London when you all came in 1917 from America. Seeing her again brought back all sorts of memories of the depressions and exaltations of other days. I think I have been both sadder and more happy since the war began than in all the other years of my life. And I used to write about the world not as it is, but about the world as I would have made it, had I been God. Now I'm trying to see things as they are, with the inevitable God shining through them. Here, at the front, God is everywhere apparent—but not the cathedral God I had imagined—not the majestic God with sublime uplifted eyes which know nothing of finite terror.

The God of the front has brave eyes which have suffered; his mouth is a human mouth, which has known the pain of parting and kisses; his hands are roughened and burnt and bloody; there is the stoop of agony in his shoulders and the hint of a valiant jest in his splendid bearing of defiance. He is one of us. He is us entirely.

He is no longer remote and eternal. For us he has again become flesh—he is our comrade; he is the man upon our left and our right hand, who goes into battle with us; he is our dead. We cannot escape him; the pettiness of our sins are forgotten in the resemblance of our neighbours to his majesty.

Now-a-days I cannot think of the poet's Christ, wandering through Galilean lilies in a woman's robes. It's his manly death, his white timeless body on the Cross that I remember. Without Calvary all his words would have been unconvincing and he himself a dreamer's fancy. It was only on the cross that Christ became flesh all that went before is like a lovely legend gradually materializing in the atmosphere of tragedy. God save us from being always happy. It's the chance of being always happy that I dread most after the war.

There's a terrible corpulence about happiness which borders very closely on physical grossness. To strive and keep on striving—that is what I want for the world when war is ended, and to have to pay with sacrifice for each advance. I don't think any of us who come back will covet virtue as our goal, save in as far as virtue embraces everything that is meant by manliness. To be virtuous in the original sense was just that—to be physically perfect.

Ah, how greedy I become out here to see some of the sudden qualities which war has called out, transplanted into the civilian world. I so fear that with peace those qualities may be debased and lost.

More than anything else the gramophone makes me remember the old days and the old aims and desires. It's the greatest miracle of the century that Caruso and Harry Lauder and George Robey, with all the best of music and laughter-makers, can step into our dug-out from the point of a needle. When we move, whatever else is left behind, the gramophone always goes. It travels in G.S. wagons, on the footboard of limbers—in all sorts of ways. We're feeling sentimental; we crank up the canned music.

Above the roar of the guns we hear, *All that I want is someone to love me, and to love me true.* We're feeling merry, so we dance to *Arizona.* All the world of forgotten pleasures can come to us through that needle-point. And I—whenever it starts—I see home pictures,—

Then in an extraordinarily poignant way I feel earnest to have lived, loved, done something big before I die. Everything already done seems insignificant and worthless. It's the feeling which you once called "divine discontent."

It's evening, as it always is when I write to you. Next door a little refugee child is chanting his prayers under the direction of his father.

One can hear the humming of planes overhead. A funny world! How persistent the religious instinct is, that men should still credit God when their hearts are bankrupt!

Goodnight, I'm going to bed now.

52

France
June 12, 1918

With me it's 6.30 in the evening. I'm sitting in a farmhouse overlooking the usual French farmyard. The chickens fly in at the window—also the cats. The window is my own mode of entrance; I feel like a burglar when I enter my "bedroom" in this fashion after midnight. Two other officers share the floor with me—literally the floor, for we use our sleeping-sacks.

There's a little boy about three, with long hair, so that at first we mistook him for a girl, who has become the temporary mascot of the battery. He carries the broken remains of a toy rifle and falls in with the men on parades, holding one of the fellow's hands. He's picked up the detail for "Shun!" and "Stand at Ease!" and carries out the orders as smartly as anyone, looking terrifically serious about it. The men call him "little sister" on account of his appearance and make him a great pet. I left him sobbing his heart out today when I had to leave him behind after he had fallen in with a squad of riflemen.

There's a genuine little girl who is our friend, of whom I am even fonder. She's a refugee kiddy of about thirteen—slim and pretty as a fairy, with a long corn-gold plait of hair down her back. As soon as we start the gramophone going she peeps noiselessly as a spirit through the window; then one of us lifts her across the sill and she sits on our knees with her face hidden shyly against our shoulders.

I'm at present reading *Gulliver's Travels.* That I should be reading them in such different circumstances from any that Swift could have imagined kindles the art of writing books into a new romance. To be remembered years after you yourself have forgotten, to have men prying into the workings of a brain which has been dust in a shell for two centuries, is a very definite kind of immortality.

To be forgotten—that is what we most dread. Never to have happened would not matter; but to have happened, to have walked the world, laughed, loved, created, and then to be treated as though we had not happened, there lies the sting of death. The thought of extinction offends our vanity; we had thought that we were of more consequence to the universe. It doesn't comfort us to be recalled impersonally in the mass, as the men who captured Vimy or thrust the Hun back from some dangerous objective. In the mass we shall go down through history, no doubt, but not as human beings—only as heroes.

We would rather be recalled by our weaknesses—as so-and-so who loved a certain girl, who played a good hand of poker, who overdrew his bank-account. Out here, from the moment a man places foot in France, the anonymity of death commences. No one cares who he was in a previous world, what he did for a living, whether he was a failure or a success. None of his former virtues stand to his credit except as they contribute to his soldier-life of the present.

None of us talk about our past; if we did, our company would yawn at us. Only the mail arriving at irregular intervals keeps us in knowledge that we once had other personalities. Letters are like ghosts of a world abandoned, tiptoeing through the dream of a sleeper. Between you and us there is a great gulf fixed—. Not that we re-sent it. Someone has to pay a price for the future safety of the world; out of all the ages we have been chosen as the persons. There is nothing to resent,—quite the contrary. Only now and then creeps in the selfish longing that we may be remembered not as soldiers, but as what we were—in our weakness as well as in our strength.

You're in a country-place where I have not been and which I cannot picture. I hope you're all enjoying yourselves. There's no need to worry on my account.

53

France
June 20, 1918

Here I am in the kind of place that William Morris wrote about. My room is in a monastery, from which all but two of the monks have long since fled. The nunnery, in which the rest of the officers are billeted, was long since vacated. A saint was born here and there used to be pilgrimages to his shrine; now only the two monks remain to toll the bell, play the organ and to go through all the religious observances. The walls of the room in which I am writing are covered with illuminated prayers.

Pinned on the door outside is the list of all the duties for the day. From my window I can see the two faithful ones pacing in the overgrown garden, counting their beads, murmuring their prayers and behaving in every way as though the war had not commenced. Such despising of external happenings, even though it be mistaken, calls for admiration of sorts.

The country is lovely and green now, all except the immediate battle-line. Birds sing, flowers bloom and fleecy white clouds go drifting over-head. One takes chance baths in chance-found brooks and the men spread their tents in the meadows. There's everything that life can offer to tempt us to go on living at present. There are moments so happy that I almost wish that you could be here to share them.

Today I'm out of touch—no letters have arrived. Perhaps they will overtake us tomorrow. A thrush is singing in the monastery garden and the slow blue twilight is falling. Mingling as an accompaniment to the song of the thrush is the slow continual droning of a plane. The reminders of war are persistent and incessant. Nevertheless, in spite of war, I found a strawberry patch this afternoon and glutted myself.

I see by today's paper that a racket has started on the Italian front. The Central Powers are declaring their weakness by striking out in too many directions. We give and we give, but we never break. We're waiting for America and her millions. How long before we can count on them to help us to attack?

It's extraordinary how the belief in America has grown. First of all we said, "She has come in too late," then, " She'll help us to win more quickly"; and now, "We need her." If America has done nothing else, she has strengthened our morale all along the line; we fight better because we know that she is behind us.

You're somewhere where the world is intensely quiet. I shall think of you where the world is happy.

54

France
June 20, 1918

I've just finished reading a big batch of mail, and have had dinner and now sit looking out on the drenched country which is covered with a shabby evening sky. In the church, which adjoins the monastery in which I stay, monks are chanting. They are always chanting. One wonders for what it is that they pray; deeds at any moment, let alone the present, are so much better. I can picture what would happen here if the Germans came. I have caught myself thinking of Marie Odelle; our scenery is similar to that pictured in the play. Strange how one goes to imagination in search of illustrations of reality!

You, at your end, seem to have been having some wildly exciting times with your processions in which the *Kaiser* has been publicly done away with. It's a phase which all countries go through, I suppose. England did at the beginning of the war. But now we entrain for the Front without bands playing and do our best not to attract attention.

We're a little ashamed of arousing other people's emotions on our behalf. All we want is a "Cheerio and God Bless You," for our goodbye. If we come back, it will be "jolly fine"; and if we don't it's "*C'est la guerre*"—we shrug our shoulders. In either event we see no reason why the feelings should be harrowed of those who stop behind.

After a series of very early morning rises, I have been picturing to myself the day when I once again wake up at the Ritz, with a camouflaged foreigner to bring my breakfast to my pillow and then leave me in peace till twelve o'clock. I wonder now why I ever left my bed in peace times and find myself marvelling at my unnecessary energy.

The French patriot who held receptions and did the business of the day while sitting in a bath of milk, had mastered the art of life. Unfortunately, if I remember rightly, he was made a glaring example of sloth by being "done in" while thus pleasurably occupied.

I'm off to do my rounds as orderly officer now. My sergeant is waiting, so, as the men say, "I must ring off."

55

France
June 23, 1918

Here I sit on a summer's evening in the red-tiled kitchen of an old farmhouse. Immediately under the open window to my right is the inevitable manure-heap—the size of which, they say, denotes the extent of the farmer's wealth. Barn-roofs, ochre-red, shine vividly in the pale gold of the sunset; at the end of the yard the walls fall away, giving the glimpse of an orchard with gnarled, lichen-covered fruit-trees. All kinds of birds are twittering and singing; house-swallows dart and dive across open spaces. In the distance the guns are booming. War affords one strange contrasts of sight and sound.

Not many of the peasants have moved away; they have great faith in the Canadians. Every now and then a forlorn group will come trailing down the road between the hedges: an old tumble-down cart, drawn by an old tumble-down horse, piled and pyramided dangerously high with old tumble-down furniture. The people who accompany the vehicle are usually ancient and tumble-down as well.

They make me recall someone's description of the Irish emigrants on the St. Lawrence, travelling with "ragged poverty on their backs." In contrast with these few straggling fugitives, hounded by avaricious fear, is the calm of a country billowy with grain and sociable with the grinning contentment of quite-at-home British Tommies.

Everything in their attitude seems to assure the French peasant, "Don't worry, old dear. We're here. Everything's all right." From barns and houses and bivouacs come the sounds of gramophones, playing selections from quite the latest musical comedies. If you wander back into the fields you will find horsemen going over the jumps, men playing baseball and cricket, officers getting excited over tennis. We even held our divisional sports the other day—and this in the midst of the war's greatest offensive.

This "'Arf a mo', *Kaiser*" attitude of the Canadians should give you some idea of the esteem in which we hold the Hun. Our backs are not against the wall. We still have both the time and the inclination to be sportsmen and to laugh.

I'm sure the enemy, grimly obsessed by the idea of breaking our line, never allows himself a moment for recreation, and I should think his balloon-observers, spying on us from the baskets of his distant sausages, must be very chagrined by our frivolity. The papers say, and very probably they're right, that German strategists are far ahead of those possessed by the Allies; but our men have learnt a trick worth all the strategy they have learnt to laugh both in success and adversity.

In this war, I believe we shall find that he who has acquired the habit of a light heart will do the laughing last. I should very much like to know how many gramophones travel with the German Tommies; hardly any, I'll bet.

They have their bands with their patriotic music, keeping always before the men the singleness of their purpose. The singleness of their purpose tires them out. On our side of the line patriotism is the last thing you hear about. Thank God, we've got time to forget it.

Whenever I start trying to explain to you the psychology of our fighting-men I'm always conscious that, even while I'm telling you the absolute truth, with the same words I'm creating a wrong impression. Fighting-men aren't magnificent most of the time; they're not idealists; they're not heroic. Very often they're petty and cynical and cowards. They're only magnificent and idealistic and heroic in the decision that brought them here, and in the last supreme moment when they bring their decision to fulfilment.

In a letter I received from Paris the other day the puzzle of the modern soldier was very well expressed. "I don't believe," it said, "I will ever get used to the courage of the men who go on and on with this terrible game. I'm thinking more now of the French and the British soldiers, who are mended up only to go at it again. I never can get used to it or take it as a matter of course.

When I think for a minute how it hurts to have a tooth filled I wonder that all the armies of the world don't get up and runaway from each other of one accord—everyone who isn't a hero or a fool, that's to say."

When I think over the problem calmly I have the same wonder. The problem was so neatly expressed that I read the passage out to the mess. They stopped in a round of poker to listen. "Well, which are we," I asked; "heroes or fools?"

"Fools," they said unanimously, and then went on playing their hands again.

They're right; we are fools. We're certainly not heroes. We're fools for a kind of kingdom of heaven's sake—but we don't act like the heaven part of it any more than we talk about our patriotism. Any mention of either would make us shudder.

I wonder what motive brought the heathen Chinee to the Western Front. I've been told that he came that he might buy food for his family, because there's a famine in China. Maybe. His bronze face stares up into ours from out the green-gold of the standing wheat stares up into ours with the inscrutable gaze of an age-old Buddha. He's the one human being on the Western Front who neither by acts nor words explains his nobility. Nobility there must have been to induce him to come; no reasoning creature would have jeopardized his body out of lust.

Last night I rode beneath a full white moon for miles through the standing crops. I only struck a road to cross it and say goodbye to it—then on and on with the soft swish of the swelling stalks against my stirrups. Shall we recall our old panics and delights if we live to reach normality again? Will normality satisfy? Shall we be content to know that all the hoard of the future years is ours? In a word, shall we ever again desire to be safe? Questions which none of us can answer!

56

France
June 27, 1918

Here's a glorious June morning with a touch of chill in the air and a jolly gold sun shooting arrows into the wheat fields. The chief sound I hear is the rattling of head-chains, for the drivers are hard at work shining up their harness. These summer days go by very pleasantly, but they throw one's thoughts back a little wistfully to the Junes of other years—especially those in which the train came skidding down the mountains from Spokane to the ranch and the lake. All day, from first waking in the morning, we begin to gamble on our chances with the mail. It arrives any time between two and five o'clock; the evening passes in reading and re-reading our letters and concocting replies. I think some letters from you are nearly due again and I'm hoping for one this afternoon.

I think I mentioned that our battery has a French baby boy of three for its mascot just at present. He has been christened Bully Beef,[1] but for what reason I don't know. Bully Beef falls in beside the sergeant major on all parades. During stables he inspects the horses, toddling round the lines and hanging on to

1. *Test of Scarlet* by Coningsby Dawson contains further information about this period and Bully Beef, and is also published by Leonaur.

the finger of an officer.

The other day he fell into the river while the horses were watering. No one noticed his disappearance for a minute or two; then he was discovered standing nearly chin-deep, doing a very quiet cry. He was consoled with pennies and I undertook to lead him up to his mother. There are many stories about Bully Beef's origin. Some say that his father is a rich Frenchman already married; others a dead *poilu*; others a sergeant of a Highland Division which was encamped in this neighbourhood. His mother is an exceedingly pretty French girl and she is not married. I can't help feeling that Bully Beef must be half British, for he isn't timid like a French child. On the contrary, he hides in the hedges and throws stones at us when he is offended and has a finely exaggerated sense of his childish dignity. What memories he'll have when he's become a man.

There was another character I mentioned in a previous letter—I called him "Battling Brown"—the chap has D. S. O.'s and Military Crosses with bars to them and delights in putting on raids. I've since found that he cuts a notch in his revolver for every Hun he has killed with it. His present weapon has eighteen notches and the wooden handle of the first is notched to pieces.

It's refreshing to find a man on our side of the line who knows how to hate. If we had hated more at the first, the war would be ended. Personally I can only hate ideas and nations-not persons; I acknowledge this as a weakness in myself.

I don't think any of us realize quite how much war has changed us, particularly in our relations to sex. Women had grown discontented with being wives and mothers, and had proved that in many departments they could compete with men. This competition was responsible for a growing disrespect. Men were beginning to treat women in a way they demanded—as though they were men.

Women were beginning to regard men with a quiet sex-contempt. It looked as if chivalry and all that made for knighthood were at an end. Then came war, calling men to a sacrifice in which women had no share—could not share because they were physically incapable of fighting—and women to the only contribution they could make, mercy and mother-hood. We've been flung back on our primal differences and virtues. War has cut the knotted sex-emancipation; we stand up today as elementally male and female as when the Garden of Eden was depopulated.

Amongst our fighting men, women actually hold the place which was allotted to them by idealists in *troubadour* times. Mothers and sisters and sweethearts, remembered at this distance, have made all women sacred. A new medievalism and asceticism have sprung out of our modern tragedy, enacted beneath the sea, on the land and in the clouds. The tragedy, while modern to us, is actually the oldest in the world—merely death.

It's evening now. No letter from home came this afternoon.

57

France
July 4, 1918

I am now attached with two guns to the infantry on a special job. I live with the battalion speak about "our battalion," in fact—and share quarters with the trench mortar officer. The country is green and fragrant with dog-roses. The dead have been gathered up and lie in little scattered graveyards. Our living men spread their blankets between the mounds and at night hang their equipment on the crosses. War robs men of all fear of the supernatural—or is it that the dead have become brothers?

One writes a description of battlefields today and it is untrue tomorrow. Everything has changed in the past year. Siege warfare, with deep trenches and guns in positions of observation, is becoming more rare; we are more mobile now and see more of the country. I believe, before many months are out, the dream of every gunner along the Western Front will have come true and we shall be firing at the enemy over open sights and coming into action on the gallop. It will be far more sporting and exciting.

The trench mortar officer with whom I am living remembers that kind of work in the early days, when my battery was still firing on the enemy while the Hun was bayoneting the batteries behind. He has a great tale of how he came right through the enemy without knowing, bringing up with him a precious load of small-arms ammunition to his general, who was cut off by the enemy. He and his five men were given rifles and together with the waifs and strays of many broken regiments held the line against the advance on Calais. Experiences such as that are worth living for; I'm hopeful that before I take off khaki I may be in something of the kind.

You needn't think of me any more at least for the present—as living in beastliness and corruption. I daresay the country where I am is almost as beautiful as where you are spending your holidays. The Hun did the Allies a good turn when he advanced, for he shoved us back out of the filth of three years' fighting into cleanness. One can see deserted cottages with their gardens full of flowers and green woods shaking their plumes against blue skies. At one of our halts the men did themselves very well with baskets of trout; they caught the trout by the simple expedient of flinging bombs into the river. The concussion killed the fish and they floated to the surface. For the present that is all my news.

58

France
July 10, 1918

I am delighted to see that every day the prophecies I made in *Out To Win* are coming true. The attack that the Americans put on on July 4th is, to my mind, one of the most significant things that has happened yet. Their battle-cry, "*Lusitania*," says everything in one word concerning their purpose in coming to France. If I were a Hun I should find it more terrifying than the most astounding statements of armaments and men. I can picture the enemy in those old shell-holes of the Somme that I know so well. It's early morning and a low white mist steals ghost-like over that vast graveyard, where crumbling trenches and broken entanglements mark the resting-places of the dead.

The enemy would be sleepy-eyed with his long vigil, but with the vanishing of night he would fancy himself safe. Suddenly, hurled through the dawn, comes the cry "*Lusitania!*" It must have sounded like the voice of conscience the old and boasted sin for which medals were struck, the infamy of which was worn as a decoration, rising out of the past to exact suffering for suffering, panic for panic, blood for blood.

Whoever chose that battle-cry was a poet—he said everything in the shortest and most rememberable way. America is in France to act as the revenge of God. She has suffered in the spirit what France has suffered in the flesh; through being in France she has learnt from the French the justice of passionate, punishing hate. I can think that somewhere beneath the Atlantic the bodies of murdered children sat up at that cry; I can believe that the souls of their mothers went over the top with those American boys. "*Lusitania!*" The white-hot anger of chivalry was in the cry.

Yes, and we, too, are learning to hate. For years we have hesitated to dogmatise as to which side God favours; but now, since hospitals have been bombed and the women who came to nurse us have been slaughtered, Cromwell's religious arrogance has taken possession of our hearts—"Let God arise, and let His enemies be scattered." When it was only we men who were wounded and killed by the Hun we could afford to regard him with an amused tolerance, but now—. This is how we have changed: we should welcome our chance to kill at close quarters and to forget mercy.

This time last year we were proud to say that we had no personal animosity for the individual German; it sounded so strong and impartial. We don't feel that way now; can't feel that way. At last, because of our women who are dead, we have learnt the magnanimity of hatred. Germany has entered a new phase of the war a phase which her persistent brutality has created. She will find no more smiling faces on our side of No Man's Land when she lifts up her hands, shouting "*Kamerad!*" We are not her comrades; we never shall be again so long as our race-memory lasts.

Like Cain, the brand of murder is on her forehead and the hand of every living creature is against her. When she pleads with us her common humanity, we will answer "*Lusitania!*" and charge across the Golgothas and the mists of the dawn, driving her into oblivion with the bayonet. No truth of the spirit which her voice utters will ever be truth for us again. It has taken four years to teach us our lesson; we were slow; we gave quarter; but we have learnt.

59

France

July 11, 1918

I've returned from being with the infantry and am back with my battery now. For the next few days I shall probably be out of touch with my incoming mail.

I have spoken several times to you about the test of war; how it acknowledges one chief virtue—courage. A man may be a poet, painter, may speak with the tongue of angels; but, if he has not courage, he is as sounding brass or a tinkling cymbal. The other day I was accidentally the witness to the promulgation of a court-martial. The man was an officer; he had been sentenced to be shot, but the order had been changed to cashiering.

There, in the sunlight, all his brother officers were drawn up at attention. Across the fields the men whom he had commanded were playing baseball. He was led out bare-headed. The sentence and the crime for which he had been sentenced were read aloud to him in an unsteady voice. When that was ended, an officer stepped forward and stripped the buttons and the badges of rank from his uniform. It was like a funeral at which his honour was buried. Under an escort, he was given "Right Turn," and marched away to meet the balance of life that remained.

In peace times he'd have been reckoned a decent-looking chap, a little smart, but handsome the kind of fellow of whom some mother must have been proud and whom probably at least one girl loved. A tall chap, too—six foot at least. I see him standing in the strong sunlight, white-faced and dumb—better dead—despised.

His fate was the fate which many of us feared before we put on khaki when the call first came. We had feared that we might not be able to stand the test and might be shot behind the lines. How and why we can stand it, we ourselves cannot say. It was all a gamble at the start. Here was one man who had failed. The arithmetic of his spiritual values was at fault: he had chosen bitter life when death would have been splendid. This must all sound very strange to you in your environment. Where you are honour and life are safe. Perhaps I should not intrude such scenes upon you.

60

France
July 15, 1918

The mail has just come up to us. The runner stuck his head into the hole in the trench where I live and shoved in a pile of letters. "How many for me?" I asked.

"All of them," he said.

I'm all alone at the battery, the major having gone forward to reconnoitre a position and all the other subalterns being away on duties—so I've had a quiet time browsing through my correspondence.

A Hun cat sits at the top of the dugout across the trench and blinks at me. We found him on the position. He's fat and sleek and plausible-looking. I can't get it out of my mind that he's kept up his strength by battening on the corpses of his former owners.

Between the guns there are two graves; one to an unknown British and the other to an unknown German soldier.

The battlefield itself stretches away all billowy with hay for miles and miles. When a puff of wind blows across it, it rustles like fire. The sides of the trenches are gay with poppies and corn-flowers. The larks sing industriously overhead and above them, like the hum of a swarm of bees, pass the fighting planes. Miles to the rear I can hear the strife of bands, playing their battalions up to the line. A brave, queer, battling world! If one lives to be old, he will talk about these days and persuade himself that he longs to be back, if the time ever comes when life has lost its challenge.

The Hun doesn't seem to be as frisky as he was in March and April. Now that he's quieting down, we begin to lose our hatred and to speak of him more tolerantly again. But whatever may be said in his defence, he's a nasty fellow. Since I started this letter I've dined, done a lot of work, watched a marvellous sunset and received orders to push up forward very early in the morning. I shall probably send you a line from the O. P. The mystery of night has settled down.

Round the western rim of the horizon there is still a stain of red. Under the dusk, limbers and pack horses crawl along mud trails and sunken roads. We become populous when night has fallen.

61

France
July 17, 1918

Tonight brought a great wad of American papers. What a time America is having all shouting and anticipation of glory without any suspicion of the cost. War's fine when it's khaki and drums on Fifth Avenue—if it wasn't tortured bodies, broken hearts and blinded eyes. Where I am the dead lie thick beneath the sod; poppies pour like blood across the landscape and cornflowers stand tall in sockets empty of eyes.

The inscription "Unknown Soldier" is written on many crosses that grow like weeds from the shell-holes. All the feet that marched away with shouting now lie silent; their owners have even lost their names. Could death do more? Where I live at present everything is blasted, stagnant, decayed, morose. War's a fine spectacle for those who only cheer from the pavement.

It isn't that I'm angry with people for seizing life and being gay. We're gay out here—but we've earned the right. Many of us are happier than we ever were in our lives. Why not? For the first time we're quite sure every minute of the day that we're do-ing right. And that certainty is the only excuse for being happy while the front-line is suffering the tortures of the damned.

I came down this morning from doing forward work; it has been raining in torrents and the trenches were awash. I sleep tonight at the battery and tomorrow I go forward again. It's re-ally great fun forward when it's fine. All day you watch the Hun country for signs of movement and snipe his support-trenches and back-country. Far away on the horizon you watch plumes of smoke trail from the chimneys of his towns, and try to guess his intentions and plans. War's the greatest game of the intel-lect yet invented; very little of its success today is due to brute strength.

It's night now. I'm sitting in my shirt-sleeves, writing by the light of a candle in an empty bottle. A row is going on outside as of "armed men falling downstairs," to borrow Stevenson's phrase. It's really more like a dozen celestial cats with kettles tied to their tails. I wonder what God thinks of it all; of all the kings, He alone is silent and takes no sides, notwithstanding the Kaiser's "*Me und Gott.*"

My jolly little major has just looked up to suggest that the war won't be ended until all the world is under arms. He's an optimist.

62

France
July 18, 1918

I'm up forward, sitting on a bank, looking at the Hun coun-try through a hedge. I know you'd give anything to be with me. In front there's a big curtain of sea-gray sky, against which planes crawl like flies.

A beautiful half-moon looks down at me with the tragic face of Harlequin. Far away across a plain furrowed by shell-fire the spires and domes of cities in the captured territory shine. Like all forbidden lands, there are times when the Hun country looks exquisitely and unreally beautiful, as though it were tempting us to cross the line.

I've just left off to watch a squadron of enemy planes which have been attempting to get across to our side. Everything has opened up on them; machine-guns are spouting their luminous trails of tracer bullets; archies are bursting little cotton-wool clouds of death between them and their desire.

They evidently belong to a circus, for they're slipping and tumbling and looping like great gulls to whom the air is native. Ah, now they've given it up and are going home thwarted. I wonder what the poor old moon thinks of all these antics and turmoils in the domain which has been hers absolutely for so many *aeons* of nights.

The horrible and the beautiful blending in an ecstasy, that is what war is today. All one's senses are unnaturally sharpened for the appreciation of both happiness and pain. You walk down a road where a shell fell a minute ago; the question always in your mind is, "Why wasn't I there?"

You shrug your shoulders and smile, "I may be there next time"—and bend all your energies towards being merry today. The threat of the end is very provocative of intensity.

It's nearly dark now and I'm writing by the moonlight. One might imagine that the angels were having pillow-fights in their bedrooms by the row that's going on in the sky. And there was a time when the occasional trolley beneath my window used to keep me awake at night!

5 a.m. The letters came last night. You may imagine the place in which I read them—lying on a kind of coffin-shelf in a Hun dugout with the usual buzzing of battened flies and the usual smell and snoring of an unwashed B. C. party. How good it is to receive letters; they're the only future we have. After I'd sent the runner down to the battery I had to go forward to a Gomorrha of fallen roofs, which stands almost on the edge of No Man's Land. Stagnant shell-holes, rank weeds, the silence of death, lay all about me, and along the horizon the Hun flares and rockets danced an impish jig of joy.

When the war is ended we shall miss these nights. Strange

as it sounds, we shall look back on them with wistfulness and regret. Our souls will never again bristle with the same panic of terror and daring. We shall become calm fellows, filling out our waistcoats to a contented rotundity; no one will believe that we were once the first fighting troops of the European cock-pit. We shall argue then, where today we strike. We shall have to preach to make men good, whereas today we club vice into stupor. We shall miss these nights.

I glance up from my page and gaze out through the narrow slit from which I observe. I see the dear scarlet poppies shining dewy amid the yellow dandelions and wild ox-eyed daisies. I am very happy this morning.

The world seems a good place For the moment I have even given over detesting the Hun. With luck, I tell myself, I shall sit in old gardens again and read the old volumes, and laugh with the same dear people that I used to love. With luck—but when?

63

France
July 19, 1918

We're all sitting round the table studying maps of the entire Western Front and prophesying the rapid downfall of the Hun. It's too early to be optimistic, but things are going excellently and the American weight is already beginning to be felt. It may take two years to reach the Rhine, but we shall get there. Until we do get there, I don't think we shall be content to stop. We may not all be above ground for the end; but people who are like us will be there.

My batman has just returned to the guns from the wagon-lines, bringing me two letters and a postcard. They were most welcome. After reading them I went out into the moonlight to walk over to the guns, and, such is the nature of this country, though the journey was only 200 yards, I lost myself. Everything that was once a landmark is levelled flat—there's nothing but shell-holes covered with tangled grass, barbed wire, exploded shell-cases and graves. I can quite understand how men have wandered clean across No Man's Land and found themselves the guests of the Hun.

I think I once mentioned the man we have cooking for our mess at present—how he was no good as a cook until I got word that his wife had been drowned in Canada; his grief seemed to give him a new pride in himself and since his disaster our meals have been excellent. This morning I found a curious document on my table, which ran as follows:—"Sir, I kan't cock without stuf to cock with."

I was at a loss to discover its meaning for some time. Why couldn't he cock? Why should he want to cock? How does one cock? And whether he could or couldn't cock, why should he worry me about it?

Then the widower presented himself, standing sooty and forlorn in the trench outside the mess. The mystery was cleared up.

The mess-cart is just up, and I'm going to send this off, that it may reach you a day earlier.

64

France
July 23, 1918

I'm sitting in my "summer-house" in the trench. One side is unwalled and exposed to the weather; a curtain of camouflage stretches over the front and disguises the fact that I am "in residence." For the last twenty-four hours it's been raining like mad, blowing a hurricane and thundering as though all the clouds had a sneezing fit at once. You can imagine the state of the trenches and my own drowned condition when I returned to the battery this morning from my tour of duty up front. It seems hardly credible that in so short a time mud could become so muddy. However, I usually manage to enjoy myself. Yesterday while at the O. P. I read a ripping book by "Q" with almost-not quite—the Thomas Hardy touch. It was called *The Ship of Stars*, and was published in 1899.

Where it fails, when compared with Hardy, is in the thinness of its story and unreality of its plot. It has all the characters for a Titanic drama, but having created them, "Q" is afraid to let them be the brutes they would have been. How many novelists have failed through their determination to be quite gentlemanly when merely to have been men would have made them famous! If ever I have a chance again I shall depict men as I have seen them out here—animals, capable of animal lusts, who have angels living in their hearts.

Today has the complete autumn touch; we begin to think of the coming winter with its drenched and sullen melancholy-its days and nights of chill and damp, telescoping one into another in a gray monotony of grimness. Each summer the troops have told themselves, "We have spent our last winter in France," but always and always there has been another.

Yet rain and mud and melancholy have their romance—they lend a blurred appearance of timelessness to a landscape and to life itself.

A few nights ago I was forward observing for a raid which we put on. The usual panic of flares went up as the enemy became aware that our chaps were through his wire. Then machine-guns started ticking like ten thousand lunatic clocks and of a sudden the S. O. S. barrage came down. One watched and waited, sending backorders and messages, trying to judge by signs how affairs were going. Gradually the clamour died away, and night became as silent and dark as ever. One waited anxiously for definite word; had our chaps gained what they were after or had they walked into a baited trap?

Two hours elapsed; then through the loneliness one heard the lagging tramp of tired men, which came nearer and drew level. You saw them snowed on by the waning moon as they passed. You saw their rounded shoulders and the fatness of their heads—you knew that they were German prisoners. Limping in the rear, one arm flung about a comrade's neck, came our wounded. Just towards dawn the dead went by, lying with an air of complete rest upon their stretchers.

It was like a Greek procession, frescoed on the mournful streak of vagueness which divides eternal darkness from the land of living men. Just so, patiently and uncomplainingly, has all the world since Adam followed its appointed fate into the fold of unknowingness. We climb the hill and are lost to sight in the dawn. There's majesty in our departure after so much puny violence.

And God He says nothing, though we all pray to Him. He alone among monarchs has taken no sides in this war. I like to think that the Union Jack waves above His palace and that His angels are dressed in khaki—which is quite absurd. I think of the irresistible British Tommies who have "gone west," as whistling *Tipperary* in the streets of the New Jerusalem. They have haloes round their steel helmets and they've thrown away their gas-masks. But God gives me no license for such imaginings, for He hasn't said a word since the first cannon boomed.

In some moods one gets the idea that He's contemptuous; in others, that He takes no sides because His children are on both sides of No Man's Land. But in the darkest moments we know beyond dispute that it is His hands that make our hands strong and His heart that makes our hearts compassionate to endure. I have tried to inflame my heart with hatred, but I cannot. Hunnishness I would give my life to exterminate, but for the individual German I am sorry—sorry as for a murderer who has to be executed. I am determined, however, that he shall be executed. They are all apologists for the crimes that have been committed; the civilians, who have not actually murdered, are guilty of thieving life to the extent of having received and applauded the stolen goods.

We had a heated discussion today as to when the war would be ended; we were all of the opinion, "Not soon. Not in less than two years, anyway. After that it will take another twelve-months to ship us home." I believe that, and yet I hope. Along all the roads of France, in all the trenches, in every gun-pit you can hear one song being sung by *poilus* and Tommies. They sing it while they load their guns, they whistle it as they march up the line, they hum it while they munch their bully beef and hard-tack. You hear it on the regimental bands and grinding out from gramophones in hidden dugouts:

Over there. Over there.
Send the word, send the word over there,
That the Yanks are coming—

Men repeat that rag-time promise as though it were a prayer, "The Yanks are coming." We could have won without the Yanks—we're sure of that. Still, we're glad they're coming and we walk jauntily. We may die before the promise is sufficiently fulfilled to tell. What does that matter? The Yanks are coming. We shall not have died in vain. They will reap the peace for the world which our blood has sown.

Tonight you are in that high mountain place. It's three in the afternoon with you. I wish I could project myself across the world and stand beside you. Life's running away and there is so much to do besides killing people.

But all those things, however splendid they were in achievement, would be shameful in the attempting until the war is ended.

Between writing this I've been making out the lines for the guns and running out to fire them—so forgive anything that is disjointed.

65

France
July 29, 1918

I have just had a very large batch of letters to read. I feel simply overwhelmed with people's affection. I have to spend every moment of my leisure keeping up with my mighty correspondence. The mail very rarely brings me a bag which is totally empty. The American Red Cross in Paris keeps me in mind continually.

I had thirty gramophone records and twelve razors from them the other day, together with a pressing invitation to get a

French leave and spend it in Paris. But your letters bulk much larger in numbers than any that I receive from anywhere else. I always leave home-letters to the last—bread-and-butter first, cake last, is my rule.

I must apologise for the slackness of my correspondence for the past few days, but two of them were spent forward while taking part in a raid, and the third at the observing post. I trained pretty nearly all the time and sleep was not plentiful. Yesterday I spent in "pounding my ear" for hours; today I'm as fresh as a daisy and writing reams to you to make up for lost time.

You'll be sorry to hear that a favourite little chap of mine has been seriously wounded and may be dead by now. A year ago, at the Vimy show, he did yeoman service and I got him recommended for the Military Medal. He was my runner on the famous day. He's been in all sorts of attacks for over three years and at last astray shell got him. It burst about ten feet away, wounding him in the head, arm and knee, besides nearly cutting off a great toe.

His name was Joy. He lived up to his name and was carried out on the stretcher grim, but bravely smiling. You can't dodge your fate; it searches you out. You wonder not fearfully, but curiously whose turn it will be next. For yourself you don't much care; your regrets are for the others who are left. Still, don't you think that I'm going west; I have an instinct that I shall last to the end.

I think I mentioned the pathetic note of the mess cook, which I found awaiting me one morning on the breakfast table: "I kan't cock without stuf to cock with." The history of our experiments in cooks would make a novel in itself.

The man before the pathetic beggar was a miner in peace times; as a cook his meals were like charges of dynamite they blasted our insides. The worst of them was that they were so deceptive; they looked innocent enough till it was too late to refuse them.

You may lay it down as final that all cooks are the dirtiest men in any unit. The gentlemen who couldn't "cock" earned for himself the title of the "World's Champion Long Distance Dirt Accumulator."

I was present when the O. C. discharged him. He sent for the man and was stooping forward, doing up his boot, when he entered. The man looked like the wrath of God—as though he had been embracing all the denizens of Hell. Without looking up the O. C. commenced, "Where did you learn to prepare all these tasty meals you've been serving us?"

"I can't cock without—"

"I know you can't cock," said the O. C. tartly; "you can't even keep yourself clean. All you know how to do is to waste good food. I'm sending you down to the wagon-lines and if you're not washed by guard-mounting, I've given orders to have you thrown into the horse-trough."

Exit the "cock."

Your letters mean so much to me. I feel that my returns are totally inadequate. Goodbye, some great news has come in and the major wants to discuss it.

66

France
July 30, 1918

I'm writing to you today, because I may be out of touch for a few days, as it looks as though I was going to get my desire—the thing I came back for. Any time if my letters stop temporarily, don't get nervous. Such things happen when one is on active service

It's about two years today since I landed in England for the first time in khaki; since then how one has changed! I can scarcely recognise myself at all. It's difficult to believe that I'm the same person. Without exaggeration, the world has become to me a much jollier place because of this martial experience. I don't know how it is with you, but my heart has grown wings. One has changed in so many ways—the things that once caused panic, he now welcomes. Nothing gives us more joy than the news that we're to be shoved into a great offensive. It's for each of us as though we had been invited to our own wedding. Danger, which we used to dodge, now allures us.

I read a very true article the other day on the things which we have lost through the war. We have lost our youth, many of us. We have foregone so many glorious springs—all the seasons have sunk their tones into the sombre brown gray mud of the past four years. We have lost all our festivals of affection and emotion. Sundays, Christmases, Easters—they are all the same as other days—so many hours useful only for the further killing of men.

"You will say," writes my author, "that the war, after all, will not last forever, and that the man and woman of average longevity will live through three-score-and-ten years of God's wonderful springs. That to a very minor extent is true. The war will not last forever; but the memory of it, the suffering of it, the incalculable waste of it, will last for all that remains of our lives-which is 'forever,' after all, so far as you and I are concerned."

He goes on to say that there are years and years—but the years in which a man and woman may know that they are alive are few—the years of love and of beauty.

I agree with all this writer says; his words voice an ache that is always in our hearts. But he forgets—life, love, youth and even beauty are not everything. The animals have them. What we have gained is a new standard of worth, which we have won at the expense of our bodies. To me that outweighs all that we have lost. I spoke to you in a previous letter of the divine discontent which goads us on, so that when we have attained a standard of which we never thought ourselves capable, we envy a new and nobler goal, and commence to race towards it. In one of Q's books I came across a verse which expresses this exactly:

O, that I were where I would be!
Then would I be where I am not;
But where I am there I must be,
And where I would be, I cannot.

Discontented, ungrateful creatures we are! And yet there is

nobility in our discontent.

By the way, over the doorway of my O. P. Is chalked this sound advice—"Do unto Fritzie as he doth unto you. But do it first."

67

France
August 13, 1918

I haven't seen a paper for nearly a fortnight, so don't know what news of the front has been published and can risk telling you nothing. Suffice it to say that I'm having the most choice experience that I've had since I took up soldiering. We are winged persons—the body is nothing; to use Homer's phrase "*our souls rush out before us.*" This is the top-notch of life; there was nothing like it before in all the ages. We triumph; we each individually contribute to the triumph and, though our bodies are tired, our hearts are elated. We'll win the war for you and bring peace back; even the most dreary pessimist must believe that now.

I try to keep notes of the tremendous tragedies and glories which I witness hour by hour, so that one day I can paint the picture for you as it happened. All day I am reminded of that motto of the Gesta Romanorum, "*What I spent, I had; what I saved, I lost; what I gave, I have.*"

So many men have given in this war given in the sense of giving all. I think it must be true of them wherever they are now, that they have in proportion to their sacrifice. It should be written on the white crosses above all our soldiers, "*What He Gave, He Has.*"

What we are trying to give is heaven to the world; it is just that those who fall should receive heaven in return.

68

France
August 14, 1918

I am writing to you in a lull—I may not have another opportunity for days. In a battle one has no transport for conveying letters only for ammunition, wounded, and supplies. I'm stunningly well and bronzed. The weather is royal and tropical and, best of all, the Hun's tail is down while ours is pointing heavenwards.

One of my gunners was complaining this morning that it was "a hell of a war." It was the smell of dead cavalry horses that nauseated him.

Another gunner cheered him up, "Where's the use of complaining, Bill? It's the only war we have."

That's the spirit of our men. It may be a hell of a war, but it's the only one we have, so we may as well grin and make the best of it. In the past few days I have seen more than in all my former experience.

I can visualise Waterloo now—and the last trump: the hosts of death deploying before my eyes. That one still walks the earth seems wonderful. God is very lenient.

But there is nothing to fear in death—only the thing that is left is horrible—and how horrible! But the things that are left are not us—we have pushed onwards to God.

69

France

August 15, 1918

I keep on dropping you little notes to let you know that everything is all right with me. It makes me very happy to hear from you; it always does, but more so than ever now-a-days.

You remember R.? A few days ago he was killed. He was just ahead of me, riding up the road. I did not see his face, but recognised his square-set figure and divisional patches. He's not had much of a run for his money, poor chap. It was his first show, but he died game.

How much longer have we got to go? It's like a long, long walk, with no mile-stones, towards an unknown destination. If we only knew how much further our goal lay, it would be easier. I dreamed last night of Kootenay, all green and cool and somnolent. It was rest, rest, rest. One gazed through the apple-trees to the quiet lake and felt happy in the too much beauty. But please don't worry about me.

70

France
August 17, 1918

I'm in the support trenches tonight carrying on with the infantry. This is my third day and I am relieved tomorrow. Yesterday I had a gorgeous spree which I will tell you about someday. I was out in front of our infantry in an attack, scouting for the enemy. This war maybe boring at times, but its great moments hold thrills which you could find nowhere else. It may sound mad, but it's extraordinary fun to be chased by enemy machine-gun bullets. I've recently had fun of every kind.

Once again death is a familiar sight tired—bodies lying in the August sunshine. In places where men once were, birds are the only inhabitants remaining.

In this hole in the ground where I am sitting I found a copy of the *New York Times* for June 30th, with the first advertisement of *Out to Win*. Less than thirty hours ago the Hun was sitting here and making himself quite comfortable. I wonder if he was the owner of the *New York Times*.

I was relieved last night, and had a difficult walk back to the battery. There were several letters from you all awaiting me. How tired I was you may judge when I tell you that I fell asleep without reading them. For the first time in a fortnight I had my breeches off last night. Up forward one got drenched with sweat by day and lay sodden and itchy on the damp ground by night. But don't think we weren't cheerful we were immensely happy. There's no game in the world like pushing back the Hun. I had another example of how we treat our prisoners. A young officer came in captive while I was shaving.

"How long before we win?" I asked him.

"We are going to vin," he replied. "If not, vhy because?"

Our Tommies started kidding him. "Say, *beau*, you don't look much like winning now."

And then they offered him water and food, although we were short ourselves and his whole deportment was insolent.

During an attack, while I was within 200 yards of the advanced post and pinned under a barrage, a Canadian Tommy wormed his way towards me.

Say, sir, are you hungry? Have some maple sugar and cake?"

Was I hungry! He had received a parcel from Canada the night before which he had taken with him into the attack. There, amongst whizz-bangs and exploding five-nines, we feasted together, washing it all down with water from the bottle of a neighbouring dead Hun.

You can't beat chaps who joke, think of home, go forward and find time to love their enemies under shell-fire. They're extraordinary and as normal as the air.

71

France
August 20, 1918

Today I have spent some time in composing recommendations for decorations for two of my signallers who were with me in my latest show. One of the lucky fellows came straight out of the death and racket to find his Blighty leave-warrant waiting for him. Not that I really envy him, for I wouldn't leave the front at this moment if there were twenty leave-warrants offered to me. I suppose I'm a little mad about the war.

I'm still very tired from my last adventure and am limping about with very sore feet—but I'm very happy. I begin to feel that we're drawing to the end of the war.

The Hun knows now that the jig is up. He was going to have defeated us this summer while the Americans were still preparing—instead of that we're pushing him back. I don't think he will gain another square yard of France. From now on he must go back and back.

This moving battle has been a grand experience; it enables you to see everything unfolding like a picture—tanks, cavalry, infantry, guns. The long marches were very wearying and we were always pushing on again before we were rested. Not that we minded—the game was too big. The first day of the attack I sailed out into the blue alone, following up the Hun. I had the huge felicity of firing at his retreating back over open sights at a range of less than 1000 yards.

We pushed so far that night that we got in front of our infantry and were turned back by enemy machine-gun fire. The Hun is a champion runner when he starts to go and difficult to keep up with. However we caught him up several times after that and helped him to hurry a bit faster. I never saw anything finer in my life than the clouds of cavalry mustering—the way the horses showed their courage and never budged for shell-fire set an example to us men. The destruction burst in the midst of them, but they stood like statues till the order was given to advance.

Then away they went, like a whirlwind of death, with the artillery following at the trot and coming into action point-blank. I came across one machine-gun emplacement that a horseman had charged.

The horse lay dead on top of the emplacement, having smothered the machine-gunner out of action. That day when I was off by myself with my two guns, I fed my horses on the oats of the fallen cavalry and my men on the rations in the haversacks of the dead. In the ripe wheat the dying stared at us with uninterested eyes as we passed. The infantry going cheering by when we were firing, waved their hands to us, shouting, "That's the stuff, boys. Give 'em hell!"

We gave them hell, right enough. I've come through without a scratch and now I'm off to bed. Don't worry if I don't write you—it's impossible sometimes and I'll always cable through London as soon as I can.

72

France
August 22, 1918

I can't sleep tonight. It's nearly one. The candle lights up the mud walls and makes the other occupants of my dugout look contorted and grotesque. They sigh and toss in their dreams. Now an arm is thrown out and a face is turned. They've been through it, all of them, in the past few days. They have a haggard look.

And somewhere in shell-holes, wheat fields, woods, they lie tonight—those others. Pain no longer touches them—their limbs have ceased to twitch and their breath is quiet. They have given their all. For them the war is finished they can give no more.

Do people at home at all realize what our men are doing and have done? Coarse men, foul-mouthed men—men whose best act in life is their manner in saying goodbye to it. And then there are the high-principled fellows from whom ideals are naturally to be expected—whatever we are, we all go out in the same way and in the same rush of determined glory. We climb the steep ascent of Heaven through peril, toil, and pain—and at last our spirits are cleansed.

I think continually of the mothers who stand behind these armies of millions. Mothers just like my mother, with the same hopes and ambitions for their sons. Poor mothers, they never forget the time when the hands that smite today were too strengthless to do more than grope at the breast. They follow us like ghosts; I seem to see their thoughts like a gray mist trailing behind and across our strewn battlefields. When the rain descends upon our dead, it is their tears that are falling. The whispering of the wheat is like the tiptoe rustling of approaching women.

Pray for us; we need your prayers—need them more than you think, perhaps. Tuck us up in our scooped-out holes with your love, the way you used to before we began to adventure. Above all be proud of us, whether we stand or fall—so proud that you will not fret. God will let us be little again for you in Heaven. We shall again reach up our arms to you, relying on your strength. We shall be afraid and cry out for your comfort. We're not brave—not brave naturally; we shall want you in Heaven to tell us we are safe.

So many thoughts and pictures come to me tonight. One is of a ravine I was in a few days ago, all my men mounted and waiting to move forward. Wounded horses of the enemy are limping through the grass. German wagons, caught by our shell-fire, stand silent, the drivers frozen to the seats with a terrifying look of amazement on their faces, their jaws loose and their bodies sagging. Others lie twisted in the grass—some in delirium, some watching.

We shall need all our water before the day is over and have no time to help them. Besides, our own dead are in sight and a cold anger is in our hearts. The stretcher-bearers will be along presently—time enough for mercy when the battle is won! We ourselves may be dead before the sun has set. I know the anger of war now, the way I never did in the trenches. You can see your own killing. You can also see the enemy's work. And yet, through it all down come our wounded, supported by the wounded Huns.

"Those chaps are very good to you," one of our officers said.

The Tommy grinned. "They have to be. If they weren't, I'd let the daylight into them. I've a pocketful of bombs, and they know it."

Well, that's one incentive to friendship, however reluctant.

The Huns are brave—I know that now. They endure tests of pluck that are well-nigh incredible. We are not defeating craven curs. I can think of no one braver than the man who stays behind with a machine-gun, fighting a rear-guard action and covering his comrades' road to freedom. He knows that he will receive no quarter from our people and will never live to be thanked by his own.

His lot is to die alone, hated by the last human being who watches him. They're brave men; they cease fighting only when they're dead.

What a contrast between love and hatred—dreaming of our mothers to the last and smashing the sons of other mothers. That's war!

73

France
August 23, 1918

Here I am lying flat on my tummy in the grass and spying on the enemy 2000 yards away. I shall be here for twenty-four hours. There's no sort of cover and the sun is scalding. Luckily we've found water in a captured village nearby and I sent our linesmen to refill our bottles. There's a lull for the moment and we stretch ourselves out in weary contentment. The body is a traitor to the spirit—it can become very tired.

I begin to see the end of the war. I can feel it coming as I never did before since I struck France. The unbelievable truth begins to dawn on me that we'll be coming back to you—that we shall wake up one morning to find that the world has no further use for our bombs and bayonets. Strange! After so much killing, to kill will be again a crime. We shall begin to count our lives in years instead of in days.

How will the pictures one's memory holds seem then? I can see, as I saw the other day, a huge German lying on the edge of a wheat field. His knees were arched. He was on his back. His head rolled wearily from side to side. The thing that fixed my attention was a rubber ground-sheet flung hastily across his stomach, whether in disgust or pity, I cannot say. I had my guns drawn up in column, my men mounted, all ready to trot into action—so I had no time for com-passion or curiosity. But from my saddle I saw an infantry-man raise the ground-sheet and underneath there was nothing but a scarlet gap. There were many sights like that that day.

There have been many since then. I have seen as many parts of the human body that the beautiful white skin tents, as a student of anatomy. What hatred and injustice has preceded the making possible of such acts!

But in these places where horrors have been committed, the birds still flit about their nests. When the tanks and the cavalry and the guns have pushed forward, nature returns to her task of beautifying the world.

How I would like to sit down and talk with you all. When the war is over I can see us going away to some quiet place and reliving the past and rebuilding the future with words. I may see you sooner than either of us expect; there's always the chance of a blighty. So far, beyond an attack of trench-fever from which I've almost recovered, I've come through scatheless.

By the time this reaches you I shall be looking forward to leave. Casualties have thinned out the numbers on the leave-list and I stand fairly high now. I ought to see England again in October.

74

France
August 30, 1918

This is only a brief note to say that all is well with me and to ask you not to worry. It's two years tomorrow since I first saw the front—two centuries it seems. I'm different inside. I don't know whether my outside has changed much—but I wish sometimes that I could be back again. I begin to be a little afraid that I shan't be recognisable when I return.

The journalists have been very free in their descriptions of our doings—they have told you everything. If I told a tithe, my letter would not reach you.

75

France
September 1, 1918

This is just another little note to let you know that I am safe and well. I am allowed to say so little to you; that's one of the worst penalties of this war—the silence. Yesterday your cable, sent in reply to mine and forwarded from London, arrived. My only chance of relieving your suspense when I have not been able to write for some time, is to get one of my English friends to cable to you.

Did you see the good news concerning R. B.?He's got his V.C. for saving life under shell-fire in Zeebrugge Harbour. His

M.L. was hit fifty times. I remember the way his neighbours used to patronize him before the war. They all laughed when he went to California to study for an aeroplane pilot. They didn't try to join themselves, but his keenness struck them as funny. What could a man who was half-blind do at the war, they asked—a man who ran his launch into logs on the lake and who crashed in full daylight when approaching a wharf?

When he had been awarded his flying certificate at the American Air School our R.F.C. refused to take him. He tried to get into the infantry, into everything, anything, and was universally turned down on the score of weak sight. His quixotic keenness made less keen spectators smile. Then, by a careless chance, he got himself accepted by the R.N.V.R. and was put on to a motor launch. Everyone pictured him as colliding with everything solid that came his way—and marvelled at the slipshod naval tests. But it wasn't his eye-sight and limitations that really counted—it was his keenness. In two years he's a V.C., a D.S.O. and a lieutenant commander. Before the war he was the kind of chap with whom girls danced out of kindness. Today he's a hero.

We were discussing him out here the other day; he's the type of hero this war has produced—a man not strong physically, a man self-depreciating and shy, a man with grave limitations and very conscious of his difference from other men. This was his chance to approve himself. People laughed that he should offer himself as a fighter at all, but he elbowed his way through their laughter to self-conquest. That's the grand side of war—its test of internals, of the heart and spirit of a man! bone and muscle and charm are only secondary.

The big things one sees done out here—done in the way of duty and so quietly! Whether one comes back or stays, the test has made all the personal suffering worthwhile—for one hour of living to know that you have played the man and saved a fellow creature's life. One never knows when these chances will come; they rush in on you unexpectedly and expect to find you ready. In the encounter the character built up in a life-time is examined and reported on by the momentary result.

And yet how one suffers for the suffering he witnesses—the suffering of horses and Huns, as well as of the men on our own side. The silent, smashed forms carried past on the stretchers; the little groups of busy men among whom a shell bursts, leaving those who do not rise. And overhead the sky is blue and the wind blows happily through the sunshine. "Gone west" that's all, to the land of departing suns. Some of us will stay to sleep among the gentlemen of France. In either event we are fortunate in having been given the privilege to serve our kind.

76

Prince of Wales Hospital, London

September 6, 1918

Here I am once again in a clean white bed with the discreet feet of nurses, like those of nuns, making hardly any sound as they pass up and down the corridor. There's just one other officer in my room. His leg is full of machine-gun bullets and, like myself, he's just arrived from France. I've not got used to this new security yet, this right to live, this ordered decency—all of which seems to be summed up in the presence of women. Less than three days ago I saw two of my gun-teams scuppered by shell-fire and the horses rolling among the wounded men. I can't get the sight out of my mind. To be alive seems an unfair advantage I have taken.—And all the time I want to be back in the thick of it. It was so glorious—such a *bon* little war, as we say out there, while it lasted.

You'll want to know what happened. On September 2nd at dawn we set out as the point of the attacking wedge to hammer our way to Cambrai. You will have read this, and more than this, already in your papers. After we had fired on the barrage for several hours, and our infantry had advanced, we began to move our battery forward by sections. The major was away on leave to Blighty, so the captain was acting O.C. He went forward to observe and reconnoitre; I was left to move up the battery. My own section was the last to move.

On the road I was met by a mounted orderly who handed

me a written order to join another battery which was doing forward work on opportunity targets. I reported to this battery and had brought my two guns into position on their right flank, when the first shell burst. The gun-teams had not unhooked; it burst directly under the centre team and scuppered the lot, wounding all the drivers and killing one of the gunners. We had got the guns into action, when another shell burst beside the left-hand gun, near which I was standing, wounding all the gun-crew except one man.

I myself got a piece in the head, between the ear and the left temple. It was a lucky chance that I wasn't killed outright. The fragment of shell struck upwards and under my steel helmet, cutting the chin-strap and the brass link which holds the strap to the helmet. It was diverted by a rivet in the strap, so instead of going straight into my head, it glanced along the skull. I was X-rayed in France and was to have been operated on, but there was no time with so many casualties coming down, so I was sent to England for the operation. I was in luck to escape so lightly. I was so grateful to my helmet that I hid it in my trench coat and smuggled it back to England with me as a curiosity—which is not allowed.

But to return to my story. After the second shell had caught us and others were popping all about us, I made up my mind that the enemy had a direct line on us. I have since been told that he put on a strong counter-attack and bent our line back for a time, so that our artillery were very near up and it's likely that he could observe us. I sent back for my teams after we had carried out our wounded, intending to drag the guns out further to the right flank. Another gun-team was scuppered and all my gunners were knocked out but three men.

The enemy now started to pay attention to my ammunition wagons, putting one shell straight in among the lot of them, so I had to leave the guns for the moment and get my wagons away. I then rode forward to where the other guns of my battery were in action and found that they had escaped casualties, so arranged to bring my guns in beside them. About an hour and a half after

I was hit I went to an advance aid-post to have my head dressed. It was just a pile of stretchers and bandages in a ditch—the living under cover in the ditch, the dead lying out on top; here a doctor and four Red Cross orderlies were working in silence. I was ordered to report at the next post back for an anti-tetanus injection, so I got on my horse and rode.

At the next post they had no anti-tetanus, so I was put on a lorry and driven back to Arras. From there I went to the casualty clearing station, where I was dressed and got two hours sleep—from there I travelled on the Red Cross train to the base, arriving at 6 a.m., only eighteen hours from the time that I was in the fighting. The hospital I went to was the Number 20 General—the same one that I was in last year. That same morning I was X-rayed and starved all day in preparation for an operation which did not happen. In the evening I was warned for Blighty, but it was the midday of September 4th before I got on the train for the port of embarkation. The journey was rather long, for I did not reach Liverpool Street till two in the morning. Yesterday, as soon as I woke up I sent you a cable.

In the afternoon Mr. W. came to see me and is coming again today. I left the front without a bit of kit, so my first S.O.S. was for a pair of pyjamas. Having studied the colour of my eyes and consulted with his lady-clerks, W. sent me a suit of baby blue silk ones with thin white stripes in them—so now I am ready to receive ladies.

3 p.m. I was X-rayed and there is a splinter between the scalp and skull. Whether the skull is fractured I don't know; I think not, however, as I feel too well. What a contrast lying here in the quiet after so many night marches, so much secrecy, such tiger pounces forward in the dawn, such agony and courage and death. There were wounded men hobbling seven miles from the Drocourt-Quéant line where I was hit, to the hospital at Arras.

The roads were packed with transports, ammunition, pontoons, rations, streaming forward, gunners and infantry marching up to the carnage with eager faces, passing the back-going traffic which was a scarlet tide of blood. It was worth living for—

worth doing—that busting of the Hindenburg Line. I hope to be patched up in two months, so that I may be in on the final rush to the Rhine. I've only been out of the fighting three days and I want to be in it again. Don't worry about me at all. I'm all right and brown and strong. Thank God I'm not dead yet and shall be able to fight again.

Note: Lieutenant Coningsby Dawson was wounded on September 2nd in the attack on the Queant-Drocourt Line, when the magnificent fighting of the Canadians broke the Hindenburg Line. The above letter describes that attack and the manner in which he got his wound.

77

London
September 8, 1918

I've returned from this offensive with a very healthy hatred of the Hun. One of our tanks, commanded by a boy of twenty, got too far ahead and was captured. When the rest of the attacking line caught up, they found him stripped naked and bound to his tank—dead. The brutes had bombed him to death mothernaked. When I tell you that no prisoners were taken for the next twenty-four hours, I think you'll applaud and wonder why the twenty-four hours wasn't extended. The men said they got sick of the killing.

Why we're decent to these vermin at all amazes me, until I remember that I also am decent to them. I think the reason is that originally we set out to be good sportsmen and are ashamed of being forced into hatred. All the way down the line the German wounded received precisely the same treatment as our own men and treatment that was just as prompt. At the casualty clearing station German officers sat at table with us and no difference was made. On the Red Cross train they were given beds in our carriage and our English sisters waited on them. I thought of how the German nurses treat our chaps, spitting into the food and the cups before they hand them to them.

Every now and then you would see a wounded Canadian

hop up the carriage and offer them cigarettes. They sat stiffly and insolently, with absurd yellow gloves on, looking as though every kindness shown was a national tribute to their superiority. There were so many of us that at night two had to lie on beds made for one. The Germans refused; they wanted a bed apiece. When they were told they would have to sit up if they would not share, they said they would sit up.

Then the sister came along to investigate the disturbance. They eyed her with their obstinate pig-eyes, as though daring her to touch them. She told them that if they wanted to sit up all night they would have to do it in the corridor, as they prevented the bed above them from being pulled down. At the end of fifteen minutes they decided to share a bed as all of us had been doing, but they muttered and grumbled all night.

There were a good many of us who wished for a Mill's bomb and an open field in which to teach them manners. It seems to me that the German is incorrigible. He was born a boor and he can never respond to courtesy. Kindness and mercy are lost upon him; he accepts them as his right and becomes domineering. If any peacemaker thinks that Christian forbearance and magnanimity will make for a new brotherhood when peace-terms are formulated, he is vastly mistaken.

The German is a bully and the only leadership that he acknowledges and the only righteousness to which he bows, is the leadership and the armed force of a bully stronger than himself. Sentimental leniency on the part of the Allies will only make him swell out his chest afresh.

You may have seen the account of a booby-trap which the Huns left behind—a crucified kitten. They banked on the humanity of our chaps to release the little beast; but the moment the first nail was drawn it exploded a mine which killed our Tommies. In contrast to this is an incident which occurred the night before our attack on the Hindenburg Line.

A hare, frightened by shell-fire, came panting through our gun-position. Some of the fellows gave chase, till at last one fell on it and caught it. It started to cry like a baby in a heart-rending sort of way.

We hadn't had very much meat and the intention in catching it had been to put it in the pot; but there was no one who could face up to killing it—so it was petted and set free again in the wheat. Queer tender-heartedness on the part of men who next morning were going to kill their kind! Their concern when the little beast began to sob was conscience-stricken and ludicrous.

78

London
September 12, 1918

I've a great piece of news for you. It's exceedingly likely that I shall visit the States on the British Mission. This must read to you like moonshine—but it's quite plausible fact. I shall not be allowed to go back to the front for two or three months, as it will probably be that time before I am pronounced fit for active service. It is suggested that during that time I come to the States to speak on Anglo-American relations. I feel very loath to postpone my return to the Front by a single day, and would only do it if I were quite sure that I should not be fit for active service again before the winter settles down, when the attack will end. I don't want to miss an hour of the great offensive.

If I agree to come to the States, I shall only do it on the pledge that I am sent straight back to France on my return. This would give me a right to speak to Americans as nothing else would. I could not speak of the war unless I was returning to it. I owe the Lord a death for every life of my men's that has been taken—and I want to get back to where I can pay the debt. But wouldn't it be ripping to have a few weeks all together again? Can't I picture myself in my little study at the top of the house and in my old bedroom! I may even manage a Christmas with you!

Having had my wound dressed and having togged myself up in my new uniform, I jumped into the inevitable taxi and went to lunch at the Ritz with some of the visiting American editors. It was delightfully refreshing to listen to Charlie Towne's wild enthusiasm for the courageous high spirits of England.

"The streets are dark at night," he said, "but in the people's hearts there is more light than ever." Two stories were told, illuminatingly true, of the way in which the average Englishman carries on. There was an officer who had had an eye shot out; the cavity was filled with an artificial one. Towne felt a profound pity for him, but at the same time he was rather surprised to see that the chap wore a monocle in the eye that was sightless. At last he plucked up courage to ask him what was the object of the monocle

The chap smiled drolly. "I do it for a rag," he said;"it makes me look more funny."

A Canadian Tommy, without any legs, was being wheeled down a station platform. Another wounded Tommy called out to him, "You're not on the staff, Bill. Why don't yer get out and walk?"

"'Cause I'm as good as a dook now," the chap replied; "for the rest of me life I'm a kerridge gent."

The thing that seems to have impressed these American visitors most of all is the way in which our soldiers make adversity appear comic by their triumphant capacity for mockery.

Towne, being a lover of poetry, was terrifically keen to visit Goldsmith's grave. I hadn't the foggiest idea where it was, but after lunch we set out in search of it. At last we found it in a shady backwater of the Inner Temple—a simple slab on which the only inscription was the name "Oliver Goldsmith." I know of only one parallel to this for illustrious brevity; a grave-stone in Paris, from which even the Christian name is omitted and on which the solitary word "Heine" is written. I liked to see the poet from Broadway bare his head as he stood by the long-dead English poet's grave.

Behind us in the temple chapel the confident *soprano* of boys' voices soared. It was a gray-blue day, made tawny for brave moments by fugitive stabs of sunshine. Lime-trees dappled the cold court-yard with shadows; leaves drifted down like gilded largesse. Old men, with dimming eyes and stooped backs, shuffled from stairway to stairway, carrying heavy ledgers. The rumble of

Fleet Street reached us comfortingly, like the sound of distant surf on an unseen shore. My thoughts wrenched themselves free from the scenes of blood and struggle in which I participated less than two weeks ago. Here, in that simple inscription, was the symbol of the one quality which survives Time's erasures—character which loved and won love intensely.

Queer letters you get from me! I write the way I feel from London or the battlefield. My room-mate is lying in bed, his poor shattered leg propped up on a pillow and a cheery smile about this lips. In the well of the hospital someone is playing-playing love-songs as though there were no war. The music, muted by distance, drifts in to me through the open window. I feel that life is mine again; I can hope. At the front to hope too much was to court disappointment. To be alive is thrilling and delicious.

79

London
October 6, 1918

It is Sunday morning. As I write the newsboys in the Strand are calling an extra-special. Before entering the Savoy for lunch I purchased a copy, which I read as I sat in the great gold and crimson lounge while I waited for a table. You know what the Savoy is like, crowded with actresses, would-be-taken-for actresses, officers on leave, chaps hobbling out of hospitals like myself, and a sprinkling of Jews with huge noses and a magnificent disregard for the fact that they are not in khaki. The orchestra was being kept up to the right pitch of frenzy in their efforts by a gentleman who is reported to get in more extra beats to the minute than any other person of his colour in London.

The feet of the girls tripped into an unconscious one-step as they entered, as though they acted independently of their owners. At the end of the rather pompous hall, with its false air of being too respectable for naughtiness, lay the terrace and beyond that the Thames, benevolent and drowsy in the October sunshine. Everything was gay and normal as though nothing except the war had happened or would ever happen. I should like Berlin to have seen us—Berlin which waited breathless for the detonation of the latest Big Bertha which she had fired on the world.

I opened my paper. Across the top of it, in one-inch type headlines, ran the message:

Germany Pleads for Peace

I am sorry to have to disappoint Germany, but the truth is I didn't blink an eyelid or turn a hair. I was scarcely mildly interested. I gazed round the crowd; their eyelids had not blinked and their hair had not turned. The *Kaiser's* Big Bertha of peace had not roused them; she must have fired a dud. Everyone looked quite contented and animated, as if the war was going to last forever.

My eye slipped down the two columns of close printing in which the mercy of the All Highest was revealed to the world. I learnt that the All Highest's new Imperial Chancellor was celebrating his new office by playing a little trick on his own credulity; he was pretending that by Christmas Germany would have sponged out all her debts of infamy with words. Prince Max of Baden was in such a hurry to bring goodwill upon earth that he had cabled to President Wilson proposals for a lasting peace; he had gone to this trouble and expense not because of anything that was happening on the Western Front, but solely "in the interests of suffering humanity." Glancing at a parallel column I read words which would have led me to doubt the sincerity of anyone less august:

Germans Defeated in All-day Battle. Tanks do Great Execution Among Hun Infantry. 1000 Prisoners Taken.

Then I turned back to see what this spokesman of a nation of humanitarians had to say for himself. I learnt that Germany had always been keen on the League of Nations: that she was anxious, as she had always been anxious, to rehabilitate Belgium; that her armies were still invincible and that the Western Front was still unbroken; that the *Kaiser* was God's latest revelation of

His own perfection and His magnanimous shadow upon earth.

Liars! Blasphemous liars! How can one treat with a nation which had not even the sense to make its shamming decent and plausible? On the Western Front today in their ignominious retreat the Germans are showing their ancient ferocity for destruction. I know, for I have just come from before Cambrai. Cities are being levelled before they make their exit; civilian populations are being carried away captive; trains piled high with loot precede their departure; they leave behind them the desolation of death. While with "incomparable heroism" their armies are executing these brutalities, their chancellor recalls us to a lost humanity and presupposes that we shall accept his professions at their face value.

I looked up from my paper at the Sunday crowd, chatting gaily as it passed through gaudy splendours into lunch. They were amazingly unmoved by anything that the German Chancellor had said. So far as their attitude betrayed them, he might never have become chancellor. If I may state the case colloquially, they didn't care a damn. There were American officers newly landed, men with the Mons ribbon, who had been in the game from the crack of the first gun, wounded Johnnies like myself, wearing the blue armlet which denotes that you are still in hospital.

One and all were seizing this jolly moment before they again caught sight of the trenches and carried on with pounding the Hun. They weren't going to spoil their leisure by discussing the perturbations of a German Chancellor.

Peace! For the Hun there shall be no peace. For him, for the next hundred years, whether we fight him or guard the wall which we shall build about him, there will be no peace. We, who have seen the mud of France grow red with blood as if with poppy petals, will never forget. That we die is nothing, provided always that two German lives pay for our death. Beyond the Rhine Germany lies intact; her towns are still snug and smiling. One journeys to them through a hundred miles of rotting corpses—the corpses of men who were our friends; yet the Imperial Chancellor appeals to our humanity and reminds us of mercy.

Mercy! While I have been in hospital several batches of returned British prisoners have arrived. I have sat at table with them, seen their neglected wounds and talked to them. One officer, in addition to his battlefield wound, has a face horribly disfigured. I scarcely know how to describe it. His jaw has been broken; his entire face has been pushed to one side. It was done by the butt of a Hun rifle in a prison hospital in Germany; an orderly woke him up by smashing his face in one morning as he lay in bed.

You may say that this was the act of one man and cannot justly be taken as representative of a nation. The time has long gone by for such generous discriminations; in four years of war-fare these ferocious cruelties have been too frequent and organised for their odium to be borne by individual men. When Germany speaks of mercy it is as though a condemned murderer on the scaffold appealed for his reprieve on the grounds of Christ's commandment, "*Love thy neighbour as thyself*" Bullies grow fluent at quoting scripture only when they feel the rope about their necks; their use of scripture phrases at the eleventh hour is proof of cowardice—not of repentance.

Judas, the front-rank assassin of all times, set an example in decency which it would behove Germany to follow, when he went out into the garden and hanged himself.

There will be sentimentalists among the Allies who will speak of forgiveness and softer judgments. Their motives will be mixed and many: some will be camouflaged pacifists; some will be influenced by personal advantages, such as relations, business affiliations and financial investments in Germany; some will be war-weary mothers and wives who will pounce on the first opportunity of regaining their remaining men. None of them will be the men who have done the fighting. Germany has turned to the American president as the intercessor for peace; the men at the front look to America to back them up in exacting the final penalty—they look to America above all the other Allies for firmness for the reason that she is not war-weary, and because millions of her men who are in khaki have yet to prove their manhood to themselves.

America beyond all Germany's adversaries came into the war on indisputably righteous grounds: we look to her to insist on a meticulously righteous settlement. In the face of the enormities which have been perpetrated by the Hun armies from the first violation of Belgium's neutrality up to now, no vengeance could be made adequate. The entire history of Germany's method of making war is one of an increasing ingenuity in devising new methods of making nations suffer while withholding the release of death.

The ravishing of women, the shooting of old men, the sending of the girlhood of occupied territories into the shame of unwilling prostitution, the wholesale destruction of all virtues that make life decent and desirable cannot be exacted as part of our penalty; but the extermination of the arch-culprits who have educated their human instruments out of manhood into bestiality can. If the *Kaiser* and the herd of human minotaurs who surround him escape the gallows, justice becomes a travesty and there is no murderer, however diabolical his atrocities, who deserves to be electrocuted.

With the turning of the tide in the Allies' favour the voice of France is already making itself heard on the side of the argument for vengeance. Whoever forgets, France has her landscapes billowed into mire by shells, her gallant cities converted into monstrous blots of brick and dirt, always to remind her. She is demanding that for every French city laid low, a German city, when the day of settlement comes, shall suffer an equal nemesis. For these crimes against civilian rights and properties, Germany has no martial motive.

They are wanton and carried out by organised incendiaries among her retreating armies, having no provocation of battle to excuse them. Moreover, as Dr. Hugh Bellot, the eminent international lawyer, has pointed out, Germany has condemned herself out of her own mouth. In her treatment, for instance, of such a city as St. Quentin, she commits three separate crimes against International law. First against the person of the civilian, second against the rights of movable property, third against the rights of public and private property.

In her own military manual, known as the *German War Book*, and regarded as her official guide for military conduct until this present war, she lays down that "the devastation of occupied territory, destruction of property, carrying away of inhabitants into bondage or captivity, and the right of plundering private property, formerly permitted, can no longer be entertained. The inhabitants are no longer to be regarded, generally speaking, as enemies and are not to be molested in life, limb, honour or freedom."

Furthermore it states that "every insult, every disturbance against the domestic peace, every attack on family honour and morality, every unlawful and outrageous attack or act of violence, are just as strictly punishable as though they had been committed against the inhabitants of one's own land." There is not a single one of the above rulings that Germany is not violating at this moment in her enforced withdrawal from France; and it is at this time that her chancellor appeals for peace in "the interests of suffering humanity."

Magnanimity! It is a fine, large-sounding word and one which it would be a disgrace to lose from our vocabulary; yet it is a word capable of much abuse if employed in our peace-dealings with the enemy. The day for magnanimity has long gone by; in being magnanimous we are unjust to both our future generations and our valiant dead. There are deeds of such vileness and treachery that they put nations, equally with individuals, outside the pale of all possible magnanimity.

For four years Germany has figured in history as a self-applauded assassin. While the role seemed to pay her, she gloried in her ruthlessness. She succeeded too well both on sea and land ever to persuade us that defeat has made her heart more tender. The only peace terms will be a carefully audited reckoning of all the happiness and innocence that she has strangled. That this may be accomplished the man at the front is willing to go on risking life and sanity for twice four years, if need be: in the certainty that it will be accomplished, he will die without regret.

We British and men of the Dominions did not always feel this way. When we entered the war we determined to remain gentlemen whatever happened. We weren't going to be vulgar and lose our tempers; we weren't going to be unsportsmanly and learn to hate. Though dirty tricks were played on us, we would still play fair. Our code of honour demanded it. There should be no retaliation. Then came the Germans' employment of gas, his flame attacks, his submarining of merchantmen, his bombing of hospitals and civilian towns.

You can't play fair with an enemy who flies the flag of truce that he may shoot you in the back. Tit for tat was the only code of honour which came within the comprehension of such a ruffian. It took three years for us to stoop to the bombing of the Rhine towns. The wisdom of the step has been proved; the children of London now sleep safely in their beds. In my opinion, at least in as far as the British armies are concerned, the success of the present offensive has just one meaning: after four years of gallant smiling our soldiers have attained a righteous anger—a determination to exact a just revenge.

They no longer make lenient discriminations between Germany and her rulers. They know now that the breath of every individual German is tainted with the odour of carnage. What makes our anger more bitter is the shame that Germany should have forced us to stoop to hatred as a weapon. But there is only one safe principle upon which to act in dealing with Germany, whether in fighting her or making peace with her: With whatever measure she metes, it should be measured to her again. Brute force is the only reasoning she understands.

The Imperial Chancellor has appealed for peace "in the interest of suffering humanity." Even in his cry for mercy he speaks vaingloriously, boasting of the "incomparable heroism" of his mob of brutes who have made humanity suffer. In not one line of his appeal is there a hint of polite regret. By the time you read this letter, this particular peace overture will be ancient history, but there will be many more of them, each one more sentimental and frantic as our armies batter their way nearer to Germany's complacent smiling towns.

As these peace overtures arrive, as they will almost daily, there is a saying of Richard Hooker's which I wish every American would repeat night and morning as avow and prayer. It is a saying which was in my mind on the dawn of August 8th, when we sailed out into the morning mist on the great Amiens attack. It is a saying which was unconsciously in the mind of every British soldier; its stern righteousness explains our altered attitude and the Cromwellian strength with which we strike.

"Lord, I owe thee a death," said Richard Hooker. Whether we be soldiers or civilians, we each one owe the Lord a Hun death for the accumulated horror that has taken place. Such blasphemies against God's handiwork cannot be wiped out with words. To make peace before the Hun has paid his righteous debt, is to shorten God's right arm and to make sacrifice seem trivial. We are not fighting to crush individuals or nations, but against a strongly fortified vileness and to prove that righteousness still triumphs in the world.

If at the first whimpering our hearts are touched and we allow the evil to escape its punishment, it will sneak off with a cunning leer about its mouth to lick its wounds into health that it may take a future generation unawares. Mercy at this juncture would be spiritual slovenliness. God has given the Allies a task to accomplish; He has made us His avengers that, when our work is ended, He may create a new heaven upon earth.

LEONAUR

ALSO FROM LEONAUR
AVAILABLE IN SOFTCOVER OR HARDCOVER WITH DUST JACKET

A HISTORY OF THE 17TH AERO SQUADRON *by Frederick Mortimer Clapp*—An American Squadron on the Western Front During the First World War.

RICHTHOFEN & BOELCKE IN THEIR OWN WORDS *by Manfred Freiher von Richthofen & Oswald Böelcke*—The Red Battle Flyer by Manfred Freiher von Richthofen and An Aviator's Field Book by Oswald Böelcke.

WITH THE FRENCH FLYING CORPS *by Carroll Dana Winslow*—The Experiences of an American Pilot During the First World War.

EN L'AIR *by Bert Hall*—The Experiences of an American Foreign Legionnaire as a Pilot With the Lafayette Escadrille on the Western Front and in the East During the First World War.

"AMBULANCE 464" ENCORE DES BLESSÉS *by Julien H. Bryan*—The experiences of an American Volunteer with the French Army during the First World War

THE GREAT WAR IN THE MIDDLE EAST: 1 *by W. T. Massey*—The Desert Campaigns & How Jerusalem Was Won---two classic accounts in one volume.

THE GREAT WAR IN THE MIDDLE EAST: 2 *by W. T. Massey*—Allenby's Final Triumph.

SMITH-DORRIEN *by Horace Smith-Dorrien*—Isandlwhana to the Great War.

1914 *by Sir John French*—The Early Campaigns of the Great War by the British Commander.

GRENADIER *by E. R. M. Fryer*—The Recollections of an Officer of the Grenadier Guards throughout the Great War on the Western Front.

BATTLE, CAPTURE & ESCAPE *by George Pearson*—The Experiences of a Canadian Light Infantryman During the Great War.

HEAVY FIGHTING BEFORE US *by George Brenton Laurie*—The Letters of an Officer of the Royal Irish Rifles on the Western Front During the Great War.

THE CAMELIERS *by Oliver Hogue*—A Classic Account of the Australians of the Imperial Camel Corps During the First World War in the Middle East.

RED DUST *by Donald Black*—A Classic Account of Australian Light Horsemen in Palestine During the First World War.